TEXAS

DAILY DEVOTIONS FOR DIE-HARD FANS

LONGHORNS

TEXAS

LONGHORNS

Daily Devotions for Die-Hard Fans

ACC
Clemson Tigers
Duke Blue Devils
FSU Seminoles
Georgia Tech Yellow Jackets
North Carolina Tar Heels
NC State Wolfpack
Virginia Cavaliers
Virginia Tech Hokies

BIG 10
Michigan Wolverines
Ohio State Buckeyes

BIG 12
Baylor Bears
Oklahoma Sooners
Oklahoma State Cowboys
TCU Horned Frogs
Texas Longhorns
Texas Tech Red Raiders

SEC
Alabama Crimson Tide
Arkansas Razorbacks
Auburn Tigers
More Auburn Tigers
Florida Gators
Georgia Bulldogs
More Georgia Bulldogs
Kentucky Wildcats
LSU Tigers
Mississippi State Bulldogs
Missouri Tigers
Ole Miss Rebels
South Carolina Gamecocks
More South Carolina Gamecocks
Texas A&M Aggies
Tennessee Volunteers

NASCAR

IN THE BEGINNING

Read Genesis 1, 2:1-3.

"God saw all that he had made, and it was very good" (v. 1:31).

The ball exploded at the first intrasquad game, but other than that, University of Texas football got off to a grand start.

Football was the new game in town in 1893 when brothers Paul and Ray McLane and James Morrison, who had all played football before, organized Texas' initial team. After a series of daily 4:30 p.m. practices, the team held an intrasquad game on Nov. 11, 1893, with help from some members of the Austin Athletic Club. Early in the game, Al Jacks, one of the non-students, was tackled, and fell on the ball, which promptly exploded. The game was delayed for about thirty minutes while a horseman rode back to town to locate a new football.

The first official opponent for the new university team was the Dallas Foot Ball Club, an experienced outfit described as "sinewy giants who have been champions of Texas since time immemorial." The university boys made a nine-hour train-trip to Dallas for the Nov. 30 game. When the players arrived, they "all bought big cigars and strutted down Main Street," reported guard Billy Richardson.

The players missed dinner when the horse-drawn rig showed up at the hotel early to take them to the fairgrounds. They made the trip escorted by an enthusiastic and noisy crowd, which

LONGHORNS

swelled to about two thousand by kickoff.

The university team scored on its first-ever possession when Morrison, a tackle, recovered a fumble in the end zone. Star fullback Ad Day kicked the two-point conversion for the early 6-0 lead. Texas would never trail. After Dallas scored to make it 6-4, Day scored twice and added the conversions. Only a late Dallas touchdown made the 18-16 final look closer than it really was.

Football at the University of Texas was under way -- big time.

Beginnings are certainly important, but what we make of them is even more important. Consider, for example, how far the Texas football program has come since that first football blew up. Every morning, you get a gift from God: a new beginning. God hands to you as an expression of divine love a new day full of promise and the chance to right the wrongs in your life. You can use the day to pay a debt, start a new relationship, replace a burned-out light bulb, tell your family you love them, chase a dream, solve a nagging problem . . . or not.

God simply provides the gift. How you use it is up to you. People often talk wistfully about starting over or making a new beginning. God gives you the chance with the dawning of every new day. You have the chance today to make things right – and that includes your relationship with God.

A lot of guys who bet against [Dallas] went out on a spree . . . that night, snapping their shirt garters at every woman they met and leaving large tips for every barbershop quartet they heard.
-- Author W.K. Stratton on Texas' first-ever football game

Every day is not just a dawn; it is a precious chance to start over or begin anew.

DAY 2

DREAM WORLD

Read Joshua 3.

"All Israel passed by until the whole nation had completed the crossing on dry ground" (v. 17b).

In the mid 1950s, he drove around Memorial Stadium and wistfully dreamed of a day when he would lead his team onto the field there. Then one night when he was in bed, a phone call came -- and so did his dream.

Darrell Royal was coaching at Mississippi State that day his wife, Edith, and he detoured through Austin to see the stadium for the first time. "I remember -- I remember *very* well," Royal said, "circling that stadium and looking at it and thinking how great it would be someday to have a chance to coach here."

Royal grew up in southwestern Oklahoma only a few miles from the Texas state line and played football for the University of Oklahoma, but his eyes were always upon Texas. When he went into coaching, the dream set in. "After I got into the coaching profession, I followed closely what was going on [in Austin]," he said. He often told Edith how great it would be to coach at Texas. He was the head coach at the University of Washington in December 1956 the night the phone call came from Texas athletic director Dana X. Bible. "Edith, this is it," he whispered.

Not yet, though. They invited him for a visit, but he was not the school's first choice. Or its 115th. The administration had drawn up a list of about 115 prospects, and Royal wasn't on it. He was interviewed because two coaches who had turned down the job said Texas would do well to talk to him. He did quite well; from interview to hiring took less than five hours.

Darrell Royal's dream was all that he could have imagined. In his 20 years as head coach (1957-1976), Texas never had a losing season, winning three national and eleven conference titles. In 1996, the university honored him by adding his name to that stadium he had driven around so many years before.

No matter how tightly or doggedly we cling to our dreams, devotion to them won't make them a reality. Moreover, the cold truth is that all too often dreams don't come true even when we put forth a mighty effort. The realization of dreams generally results from a head-on collision of persistence and timing.

But what if our dreams don't come true because they're not the same dreams God has for us? That is, they're not good enough and in many cases, they're not big enough.

God calls us to great achievements because God's dreams for us are greater than our dreams for ourselves. Could the Israelites, wallowing in the misery of slavery, even dream of a land of their own? Could they imagine actually going to such a place?

The fulfillment of such great dreams occurs only when our dreams and God's will for our lives are the same. Our dreams should be worthy of our best – and worthy of God's involvement in making them come true.

I used to daydream about what it'd be like to coach at Texas.
-- Darrell Royal

If our dreams are to come true, they must be worthy of God's involvement in them.

CELEBRATION TIME

Read Luke 15:1-10.

"There is rejoicing in the presence of the angels of God over one sinner who repents" (v. 10).

The pitcher who saved the game was rammed in the midsection. Another Longhorn baseball player was cleated in the face. But it wasn't a brawl; it was just a more-than-slightly exuberant celebration of a national championship.

On Sunday, June 26, 2005, the Horns threw an impromptu dog-pile after they finished sweeping Florida to win the sixth national title in school history. Relief pitcher J. Brent Cox struck out the last Gator batter to secure the 6-2 win that came on the heels of the 4-2 victory over Florida the day before. All-tourney catcher Taylor Teagarden then started the celebration when he plowed into Cox, hitting him harder than any opposing team had during the entire CWS. Cox tied a world series record with five appearances. He pitched 10.1 innings and did not give up an earned run.

Third baseman David Maroul was named the Most Outstanding Player in Omaha. His three-run homer in the sixth put the Longhorns up 6-0 in the deciding game. Maroul hit .500 for the series (8 for 16) with two homers and eight RBIs. In addition to sweeping the Gators, Texas beat Baylor 5-1, Tulane 5-0, and Baylor 4-3. The national champions finished the season at 56-16 to hand coach Augie Garrido his second UT title.

The save was Cox's 24th of the season, and when he struck out the final batter, he dropped to his knees and pounded the dirt with both hands. Just as he was rising to his feet, Teagarden came running. The dogpile was under way.

Freshman backup catcher Todd Gilfillan emerged from all the mayhem with his face and uniform bloodied by small cuts over his right eye and on his right cheek. A teammate's cleat-laden feet had had a close encounter with his head. He bore those souvenirs of the celebration with a broad smile.

Texas just won another national championship. You got that new job or that promotion. You just held your newborn child in your arms. Life has those grand moments that call for celebration. You may jump up and down and scream in a wild frenzy or share a quiet, sedate candlelight dinner at home -- but you celebrate.

Consider then a celebration that is beyond our imagining, one that fills every niche and corner of the very home of God and the angels. Imagine a celebration in Heaven, which also has its grand moments.

Those grand moments are touched off when someone comes to faith in Jesus. Heaven itself rings with the joyous sounds of the singing and dancing of the celebrating angels. Even God rejoices when just one person – you or someone you have introduced to Christ? -- turns to him.

When you said "yes" to Christ, you made the angels dance.

Teabag [Taylor Teagarden] really drilled me good.
-- J. Brent Cox on the championship celebration

God himself joins the angels in heavenly celebration when even a single person turns to him through faith in Jesus.

IN THE KNOW

Read John 4:19-26, 39-42.

"They said to the woman, . . . 'Now we have heard for ourselves, and we know that this man really is the Savior of the world'" (v. 42).

Texas defensive end Brian Robison just knew. The eventual result was a win in what is often called the greatest game in college football history. And that win meant a national championship.

On Jan. 4, 2006, in the Rose Bowl, the Trojans from Southern California were two yards away from winning their 35th straight game and a third consecutive national title. They sat at the Texas 45 facing fourth and two with a 38-33 lead and less than three minutes to play. "I remember all of us just looking at each other and saying, 'This is it,'" recalled Robison, a junior who was first-team All-Big 12 that season. Everybody in the world who was watching knew that if Southern Cal made a first down, the title was theirs.

When the Trojans broke their huddle, Robison settled into his stance and tried to block everything about the play's implications out of his mind. Instead, he concentrated on what he saw across the line of scrimmage -- and what he saw was USC running back LenDale White, who had already rushed for 123 yards and three touchdowns. And Robison knew what was coming.

Because he knew what to look for, Robison made a move that he wasn't supposed to: He stunted by cutting to the inside. "I kind of saw an opening there," he said. "I ended up slipping through." And what he found when he slipped through was exactly what he had known was coming: White with the ball. Robison made first contact, grabbed an ankle, and held on for help to arrive. White went down a yard short of the first down.

History, of course, has recorded quite voluminously that Vince Young scored the game-wining touchdown on fourth-and-five with 19 seconds left to play. Everybody knows that. But Young got the chance to make that historic run only because of what Brian Robison knew on that critical fourth-down play.

Robison just knew in the same way you know certain things in your life. That your spouse loves you, for instance. That you are good at your job. That tea should be iced and sweetened. That a bad day fishing is still better than a good day at work. That the Longhorns had that win over USC all the way. You know these things even though no mathematician or philosopher can prove any of this on paper.

It's the same way with faith in Jesus: You just know that he is God's son and the savior of the world. You know it in the same way that you know Texas is the only team worth pulling for: with every fiber of your being, with all your heart, your mind, and your soul.

You just know, and because you know him, Jesus knows you. And that is all you really need to know.

I saw it. Read it.
-- Brian Robison on the fourth-down stop of USC

A life of faith is lived in certainty and conviction:
You just know you know.

A RIPE OLD AGE

Read Psalm 92.

"[The righteous] will still bear fruit in old age, they will stay fresh and green, proclaiming, 'The Lord is upright'" (vv. 14-15).

Kearie Lee Berry did what many Texas football players have done; he made all-conference. What made him different, however, was that he was 32 years old when he did it.

Berry was a true University and American hero. He lettered in football at Texas in 1912, '14, and '15 and in track and wrestling in 1915 and '16. Berry was a junior with a year of eligibility left when World War I interrupted his plans. The Texas National Guard called him to active duty, and he served in France. After the war, he played some football for an Army all-star team until in 1924 he decided to finish his degree at Texas.

After he graduated from Texas, Berry returned to duty with the Army and became one of World War II's most decorated officers. He led the First and Third Infantry Divisions in the Battle of Bataan, was the last officer in the Philippines to surrender his command to the Japanese, and was part of the infamous Bataan Death March. He even carried a comrade on the forced march to POW camps. Berry was incarcerated for forty months before the Allies freed him in 1945.

With all that, what Berry did in his one year at Texas (1924) after World War I was perhaps his most incredible achievement.

He was 32, married, the father of three children, and had a knee injury. Nevertheless, he decided to use the one year of eligibility he had left and went out for the team. He not only made it, but he was named All-Southwest Conference as a guard, a full twelve years after he first suited up for the Horns. In 1959, he was inducted into the Longhorn Hall of Honor.

While 32 is a rather ripe old age to be playing college football, we live in a youth-obsessed culture that idolizes the young. We don't like to admit – even to ourselves – that we're not as young as we used to be.

So we keep plastic surgeons in business, dye our hair, buy cases of those miracle wrinkle-reducing creams, and redouble our efforts in the gym. Sometimes, though, we just have to face up to the cold, hard truth the mirror tells us every time it speaks to us: We're getting older every day.

It's really all right, though, because aging and old age are part of the natural cycle of our lives, which was God's idea in the first place. God's conception of the golden years, though, doesn't include unlimited close encounters with a rocking chair and nothing more. God expects us to serve him as we are able all the days of our life.

Those who serve God flourish no matter their age because the energizing power of God is in them.

Very few thought [K.L. Berry] would be able to stand up to the strenuous grind [Coach E.J.] Stewart puts his youngsters through.
                                                                    -- The Alcade

**Servants of God don't ever retire; they keep
working until they get the ultimate promotion.**

BLESS YOU

Read Romans 5:1-11.

"We also rejoice in our sufferings because we know that suffering produces perseverance; perseverance, character; and character, hope. And hope does not disappoint us" (vv. 3-5a).

Laura Wilkinson regarded a broken foot as a blessing.

Wilkinson has been called "one of the most revered divers in Texas history." She won the NCAA platform championship as a freshman in 1997 and again as a junior in 1999. "I still bleed burnt orange," she said in 2009 upon the occasion of her induction into the Longhorn Hall of Honor. "I very much cherish my two NCAA titles . . . because I just loved being a Longhorn."

Wilkinson's dazzling smile belied a competitive drive that let her find blessings in all aspects of her sport. "There's nothing like overcoming something that scares you so much," like diving off a platform, she said. "Nothing feels better." If she says so.

While she was practicing in March before the 2000 Olympics in Sydney, Wilkinson broke a foot in three places. The result was a piece of bone that floated to the bottom of her foot and "felt like I was walking on a rock everywhere." And Wilkinson regarded that as a blessing? She said the injury forced her to intensify her focus on her goal of reaching the Olympics.

Despite the floating bone, she was in first place in Sydney as she prepared for her most difficult dive, the one she had been practicing when she broke her foot. Her coach, Kenny Armstrong, had some encouragement for her. He told her, "Do it for Hilary." Hilary Grivich had been Wilkinson's friend and Longhorn teammate who was killed in an auto accident in 1998.

"Everything clicked," she said. It "wasn't about winning anymore. It was about the journey." That journey became one of the great blessings of Wilkinson's life. She recited her favorite Bible verse (Phil. 4:13), nailed the dive, and won the gold medal.

We just never know what God is up to. We can know, though, that he's always busy preparing blessings for us and that if we trust and obey him, he will pour out those blessings upon us.

Some of those blessings, however, come our way rather deftly disguised as some form of hardship and suffering, as was the case with Laura Wilkinson. It is only after we can look back upon what we have endured that we understand it as a blessing.

The key lies in trusting God, in realizing that God isn't out to destroy us but instead is interested only in doing good for us, even if that means allowing us to endure the consequences of a difficult lesson. God doesn't manage a candy store; more often, he relates to us as a stern but always loving father.

If we truly love and trust God, no matter what our situation is now, he has blessings in store for us. This, above all, is our greatest hope.

When I broke my foot, it was like windshield wipers and my vision became very clear again.
— Laura Wilkinson on finding a blessing in an injury

Life's hardships are often transformed into
blessings when we endure them trusting in God.

THE MOTHER LODE

Read John 19:25-30.

"Near the cross of Jesus stood his mother" (v. 25).

She never worked a day for the University of Texas, nor did she ever win any awards or honors from the school. Yet, upon her death in 2009, she was remembered as "one of the most important women in the history of Texas Longhorns football." She was Ann Campbell, who had a son named Earl.

Earl Campbell's "high school career [in the early 1970s] . . . was the stuff from which legends are made. He was, to those who saw him, the greatest high school running back in state history." College recruiters from all over the country came calling in 1974, and they all had to go through Ann Campbell.

She was a woman of steely integrity and unwavering faith who raised Earl and his ten siblings by growing and selling roses after their dad died in 1966. In an age when illegal recruiting offers were routine, she "would stand in the doorway" and turn them aside. Her son would say he was not for sale: "My people have been bought and sold long enough."

UT assistant coach Ken Dabbs was present for one of the most momentous moments in Texas football history, the evening Ann Campbell made her decision. The stress from the unrelenting harassment by the recruiters finally drove her blood pressure high enough to send her to bed. As Dabbs was about to leave one evening, a phone caller asked if Oklahoma's Barry Switzer could come for a visit. "She raised up and looked Earl straight in the eye," Dabbs recalled. "This has gone on long enough," she said. "You know you are going down to Texas with Coach Dabbs and Coach Royal, so you tell them that."

The rest, of course, is football history. After he won the 1977 Heisman Trophy and turned pro, Earl Campbell built his mother a house, so, he said, "she wouldn't have to look at the stars at night through the holes in the roof."

Mamas often know what is best for their children. No mother in history, though, has faced a challenge to match that of Mary, the teenaged peasant girl whom God chose to be the mother of Jesus. Like mamas and their children throughout time, Mary experienced both joy and perplexity in her relationship with her son.

To the end, though, Mary stood by her boy. She followed him all the way to his execution, an act of love and bravery since Jesus was condemned as an enemy of the Roman Empire.

But just as mothers such as Mary, Ann Campbell, and perhaps yours would apparently do anything for their children, so will God do anything out of love for his children. After all, that was God on the cross at the foot of which Mary stood, and he was dying for you, one of his children.

Earl Campbell is the greatest football player I have ever seen, and Ann Campbell is the best coach there ever was.

– Fred Akers

Mamas often sacrifice for their children, but God, too, will do anything out of love for his children, including dying on a cross.

CLOCKWORK

Read Matthew 25:1-13.

"Keep watch, because you do not know the day or the hour" (v. 13).

The clock ticked down to zero, but the Longhorns still had time to win the Big 12 championship.

"It was high drama at Cowboys Stadium" on Dec. 5, 2009, when the Longhorns and the Cornhuskers met in Arlington in the Big 12 Conference championship. With only 1:44 to play, Nebraska kicked a 42-yard field goal to lead favored Texas 12-10.

After the kickoff, quarterback Colt McCoy hit wide receiver Jordan Shipley with a 19-yard completion. A personal-foul penalty on the tackle moved the ball to the Nebraska 26. A sack and a one-yard loss set up a third down with about 15 seconds on the clock.

As the final seconds ticked away, McCoy straightened up and sailed the ball out of bounds. And the clock ticked down to 0:00. For a "brief, scary moment," the game was over. The Cornhuskers even stormed onto the field in celebration.

Had the most successful quarterback in Texas history committed a major blunder in his next-to-last game? McCoy was sure he hadn't, that time still remained on the clock. In fact, he was so sure of it that he had been surprised when the officials signaled that the game was over. He was right. The refs reviewed the play -- slowing time down -- and put one second back on the clock. The review, said the conference's director of officials after the game, allowed the crew "to correct an 'egregious' clock error."

That left the Horns' conference and national title hopes riding on the foot of Hunter Lawrence, a senior who had never kicked a game-winning field goal. Nebraska called a time out, giving Lawrence extra time to think about it, but his holder, Shipley, was up to the moment. He quoted Jeremiah 17:7 to his kicker: "Blessed is the man who trusts in the Lord, whose confidence is in him."

Lawrence's 46-yard kick was good, and this time there really was no time left on the clock.

We may pride ourselves on our time management, but the truth is that we don't manage time; it manages us. Hurried and harried, we live by schedules that seem to have too much what and too little when. By setting the bedside alarm at night, we even let the clock determine how much down time we get. A life of leisure actually means one in which time is of no importance.

Every second of our life – all the time we have – is a gift from God, who dreamed up time in the first place. We would do well, therefore, to consider what God considers to be good time management. After all, Jesus himself warned us against mismanaging the time we have.

From God's point of view, using our time wisely means being prepared at every moment for Jesus' return, which will occur -- well, only time will tell when.

I think in Lincoln, it'll be the clock. And in Austin, it'll be the comeback.
– Mack Brown on how the 2009 title game will be remembered

We mismanage our time when we fail
to prepare for Jesus' return even though
we don't know when that will be.

ANGER MANAGEMENT

Read James 1:19-27.

"Everyone should be quick to listen, slow to speak and slow to become angry, for man's anger does not bring about the righteous life that God desires" (vv. 19-20).

The Texas women's basketball team of 1985-86 was an angry bunch. That anger fueled a run all the way to an undefeated season and the national championship.

The anger stemmed from the way the 1984-85 season ended. The Longhorns were ranked No. 1, and the Final Four was held in Austin. "We were supposed to win the whole thing," said head coach Jody Conradt. "It [was] all set up for us." But Western Kentucky upset the Horns at the buzzer in the NCAA regionals. The result? "It made us mad," said point guard Kamie Ethridge.

The squad of 1985-86 returned all five starters from the powerhouse team of the season before. Three players -- Ethridge, Fran Harris, and Andrea Lloyd -- were on everyone's pre-season All-America team. Ethridge would win the Wade Trophy as the national player of the year. Fifth-year senior center Annette Smith would finish her career as the top scorer in Texas women's history, a record she still holds. Thus, the team had both the talent and an attitude born of their anger.

As expected, the Longhorns breezed through their conference schedule. They then exacted their revenge on Western Kentucky in the Final Four. Behind freshman forward Clarissa Davis' 32 points and 18 rebounds, the Horns blasted the Hilltoppers 90-65. They then topped off a 34-0 season with a 97-81 crushing of USC and legendary player Cheryl Miller behind 24 points and 12 rebounds from Davis, the tournament MVP.

The angry Longhorns were the first women's team in NCAA history to go undefeated.

Our society today is well aware of anger's destructive power because too many of us don't channel our anger constructively as the national champions of 1986 did. Anger is a healthy component of a functional human being until – like other normal emotions such as fear, grief, and worry – it escalates out of control. Anger abounds when Texas loses or we are particularly frustrated. The trouble comes when that anger intensifies from annoyance and disappointment to rage and destructive behavior.

Anger has both practical and spiritual consequences. Its great spiritual danger occurs when anger is "a purely selfish matter and the expression of a merely peevish vexation at unexpected and unwelcome misfortune or frustration." When that happens, anger interferes with the living of the righteous, Christ-like life God intends for us.

Our own anger, therefore, can incur God's wrath; making God angry can never be anything but a perfectly horrendous idea.

When you get angry and start shouting, nothing good ever really happens.

-- Olympic rower Michelle Guerette

**Anger becomes a problem when it escalates
into rage and interferes with the righteous life
God intends for us.**

MAKE NO MISTAKE

Read Mark 14:66-72.

"Then Peter remembered the word Jesus had spoken to him: 'Before the rooster crows twice you will disown me three times.' And he broke down and wept" (v. 72).

For two years, Bobby Layne seethed over a mistake he had made. He finally got the chance to rectify it -- and did he ever!

Layne, of course, is a Longhorn legend, a member of both the NFL and the Texas Longhorn halls of fame. He actually came to Austin as a baseball recruit. He missed part of the 1945 season in the merchant marine but returned to lead the Horns to a strong 9-1 finish that landed them in the Cotton Bowl.

He was spectacular that New Year's Day in Dallas, accounting for every Longhorn point in a 40-27 win over Missouri. He ran for three touchdowns, caught a 50-yard pass for another, completed passes for the other two, and kicked four extra points. When he finished up in 1947, Layne owned every passing record in school history. He kept the school record for quarterback wins (28) until Vince Young broke it.

In 1944, Oklahoma State (then Oklahoma A&M) beat Layne and the Horns 13-8. Layne threw an ill-advised interception in the game that helped A&M erase an 8-0 Texas lead. In a local barber shop a few days after the game, a Longhorn fan was dissecting the loss, declaring Layne "just shouldn't have thrown the ball." From the chair next to him, Layne jumped up, pulled a towel off his face, glared at the fan, and said, "Listen, pal. You've had a whole weekend to think about this. If I had had that much time, I wouldn't have thrown the ball, either."

Layne made up for his mistake in 1946 in the nation's "game of the week." A&M hadn't lost to a college team in two seasons and scored first on a short drive set up by -- of all things -- a Layne interception. But after that, Layne scored four touchdowns rushing before the third quarter was over; the Horns buried A&M 54-6.

It's distressing but it's true: Like the great quarterbacks and Simon Peter, we all make mistakes. Only one perfect man ever walked on this earth, and no one of us is he. Some mistakes are just dumb. Like locking yourself out of your car or falling into a swimming pool with your clothes on. Other mistakes are more significant. Like heading down a path to addiction. Committing a crime. Walking out on a spouse and the children.

All these mistakes, however, from the momentarily annoying to the life-altering tragic, share one aspect: They can all be forgiven in Christ. Other folks may not forgive us; we may not even forgive ourselves. But God will forgive us when we call upon him in Jesus' name.

Thus, the twofold fatal mistake we can make is ignoring the fact that we will die one day and subsequently ignoring the fact that Jesus is the only way to shun Hell and enter Heaven. We absolutely must get this one right.

I try not to make the same mistakes today that I made yesterday.
-- Darrell Royal

Only one mistake we make sends us to Hell
when we die: ignoring Jesus while we live.

THE PRIZE

Read Philippians 3:10-16.

"I press on toward the goal to win the prize for which God has called me heavenward in Christ Jesus" (v. 14).

Beau Trahan won one of the most cherished of the Longhorn football post-season awards -- and he gave it away.

From 1999-2002, Trahan played in 52 games, mostly as one of the best special-teams players in Texas history. He was the Special Teams MVP each of his last three seasons. As a senior, he successfully converted three fourth-down fake field goals, including a 24-yard TD against Houston, the last of his three career scores.

Trahan was among the Texas players most actively involved in the team's community service programs. In the spring of 2001, he first heard the story of Archer Hadley, a 5-year-old with cerebral palsy. While the other kids played games, Archer sat alone in his wagon and watched. As Archer's father put it, "The teachers did everything they could for him, but he was too heavy for them to carry around all the time."

And then one day, Archer's new friend showed up. Trahan was that new friend, and instantly, "the little boy who couldn't walk was the hit of the school." When the kids played football, tag, or whatever, Archer Hadley entered the game riding on the strong, broad shoulders of Beau Trahan. "Beau became not only Archer's inspiration, he became his legs," said Archer's dad.

Trahan showed up twice a week until Archer entered kindergarten and his schedule changed. Still, Trahan stayed in touch with Archer. For the football banquet of Friday, Dec. 15, 2001, Trahan's parents stayed with Archer's folks. They came to see their son win the Coca-Cola Community Service Award, one of the prizes most cherished and appreciated by the players.

Beau Trahan didn't keep his trophy long. Saturday morning, he went to the Hadley home and gave it to Archer.

Even the most modest and self-effacing among us can't help but be pleased by prizes and honors. They symbolize the approval and appreciation of others, whether it's an All-American team, an Employee of the Month trophy, a plaque for sales achievement, or the sign declaring yours as the neighborhood's prettiest yard.

Unlike Beau Trahan's situation, such prizes and awards are often the culmination of the pursuit of personal achievement and accomplishment. Nothing is inherently wrong with any of that as long as we keep such recognition in perspective.

That is, we must never let awards become such idols that we worship or lower our sight from the greatest prize of all and the only one truly worth winning. It's one that won't rust, collect dust, or leave us wondering why we worked so hard to win it in the first place. The ultimate prize is eternal life, and it's ours through Jesus Christ.

A gold medal is a wonderful thing, but if you're not enough without it, you'll never be enough with it.
-- *John Candy in* Cool Running

The greatest prize of all doesn't require competition to claim it; God has it ready to hand to you through Jesus Christ.

A SECOND CHANCE

Read John 7:53-8:11.

"'Then neither do I condemn you,' Jesus declared. 'Go now and leave your life of sin'" (v. 8:11).

Lauren Dickson figured it was all over -- and then a bum ankle gave her a second chance.

Dickson was one of the University of Virginia's most successful volleyball players. Though she was from Austin, she wasn't recruited by the Longhorns out of high school. A team MVP and captain for the Cavaliers as a senior in 2009, she finished No. 13 on the school's all-time kills list. An outside hitter, she had played three years for UVa and had earned her degree when the 2009 season ended. The part of her life that included volleyball was over -- or at least that's what Dickson thought.

But midway through her sophomore season of 2007, she had suffered an ankle injury that allowed her to take a medical redshirt. She didn't expect to use it after earning her degree at UVa, but then she was accepted into graduate school at Texas. With that one year of eligibility left, she figured she might as well give Longhorns head coach Jerritt Elliott a call to see if he had need of another body to help the squad at practices. "I didn't think I'd ever play," Dickson said. "I thought maybe being a practice player two or three times a week."

Elliott liked what he heard and asked her to walk on and try for a spot on the roster. Dickson saw she had a second chance not only to play some more but to reach the NCAA Tournament, a goal that had eluded her at UVa. She soon moved from the equivalent of a scout team member to a valuable member of the team, even starting some. In the win over Purdue in the Austin regional final, she led the team with twelve digs.

"She's a great story," Elliott said about Dickson's making the most of her second chance. She didn't just practice; she played extensively; she didn't just make a trip to the NCAA Tournament; she helped the 2010 team romp all the way to the Final Four.

"If I just had a second chance, I know I could make it work out." Ever said that? If only you could go back and tell your dad one last time you love him, take that job you passed up rather than relocate, or replace those angry shouts at your son with gentle encouragement. If only you had a second chance, a mulligan.

As the story of Jesus' encounter with the adulterous woman illustrates, with God you always get a second chance. No matter how many mistakes you make, God will never give up on you. Nothing you can do puts you beyond God's saving power. You always have a second chance because with God your future is not determined by your past or who you used to be. It is determined by your relationship with God through Jesus Christ.

God is ready and willing to give you a second chance – or a third chance or a fourth chance – if you will give him a chance.

I have to thank God for giving me the gift that he did as well as a second chance for a better life.
-- Olympic figure skating champion Oksana Baiul

You get a second chance with God
if you give him a chance.

CHOICES

Read Deuteronomy 30:15-20.

"I have set before you life and death, blessings and curses.
Now choose life, so that you and your children may live"
(v. 19).

Would you choose to give up what you love most and in return save any number of lives? Matt Nader, who had no choice,
wouldn't have made that decision at the time. But today?

On Nov. 25, 2010, twenty Longhorn seniors celebrated their last
home football game. At one time in his life, Nader would have
been No. 21, but he wasn't. "My dream was taken away from me,"
he said shortly before the season ended, "without me being able
to fight for it."

In 2006, Nader was a high-school offensive lineman and a four-
star Texas recruit. During a game, he collapsed; he quit breathing;
his heart stopped. A cardiologist saved his life with a defibrillator, and three days later one was installed in his chest. Nader was
told he could never play football again.

The Longhorns honored their scholarship offer and took Nader
on as a student assistant, which allowed him to be around and
involved with football without playing the game. Still, he wondered. He felt strong, fast, invincible. What if his incident had just
been a fluke, a one-time deal?

So one afternoon during an unofficial workout with the Texas
offensive line, he ran some sprints. Quickly, his vision blurred,

and, as he put it, "Everything kind of started to cave in." The internal defibrillator did its job, saving his life. But Nader no longer wondered whether he could still play football. He knew.

That certainty changed him and his life. He became the face and the voice of a cause, speaking everywhere about the importance of defibrillators. He shared his testimony with state lawmakers, and the Senate passed a bill requiring schools to have them.

Nader once said he doubted that back in 2006 he would have voluntary chosen the path his life took. But now? "If I could go back and change it," he said, "I'd have to say no."

Your life is the sum of the choices you've made. That is, you have arrived at this moment and this place in your life because of the choices you made in your past. Your love of the Longhorns. Your spouse or the absence of one. Mechanic, teacher, or beautician. Condo in downtown Houston or ranch home outside Fort Worth. You chose; you live with the results.

That includes the most important choice you will ever have to make: faith or the lack of it. That we have the ability to make decisions when faced with alternatives is a gift from God, who allows that faculty even when he's part of the choice. We can choose whether or not we will love him. God does remind us that this particular choice has rather extreme consequences: Choosing God's way is life; choosing against him is death.

Life or death. What choice is that?

The choices you make in life make you.

-- John Wooden

**God gives you the freedom to choose: life or death;
what kind of choice is that?**

VIRTUAL REALITY

Read Habakkuk 1:2-11.

"Why do you make me look at injustice? Why do you tolerate wrong? Destruction and violence are before me; there is strife, and conflict abounds" (v. 3).

Whatever Texas' Emmett "Duke" Carlisle was doing out there right in front of about 75,000 folks sure didn't look too good; even a ref said so. Fortunately, reality wasn't what it appeared to be.

As a senior quarterback, Carlisle outdueled Navy's Heisman-Trophy winner, Roger Staubach, in the 1964 Cotton Bowl for the national-champion Longhorns. In the game's first 40 minutes, Carlisle, who had thrown only one touchdown pass all season in Darrell Royal's ground-oriented offense, completed seven passes for 212 yards and two touchdowns. He was also the game's leading rusher with 54 yards and a third score. Texas won 28-6.

As a junior, Carlisle led the 1962 squad to the championship of the Southwest Conference and the Cotton Bowl. In that 1963 bowl game, Carlisle at one point appeared to behave in somewhat of a lewd manner. During the game, he found a 50-cent piece on the field and stuck it in his pants. Playing in the defensive backfield, Carlisle later ended up in a pileup and suddenly felt excruciating pain in his thigh. He realized that the coin was being ground into his flesh. He started kicking people and screaming in a desperate effort to get out of the mass of humanity.

Eventually back on his feet, Carlisle reached into his pants to retrieve the offending coin but managed to push it farther down. "At about the 50-yard line in front of 75,000 people, I had my entire right arm jammed down into the leg of my pants," Carlisle said. A concerned official came over and asked, "You got a problem there, son?" "I will be OK in a minute," Carlisle responded. "I sure hope so," the ref replied, "because that doesn't look real good."

No, it didn't, but it really wasn't what it seemed.

Sometimes in life things aren't what they seem. In our violent and convulsive times, we must confront the possibility of a new reality: that we are helpless in the face of anarchy; that injustice, destruction, and violence are pandemic in and symptomatic of our modern age. Anarchy seems to be winning, and the system of standards, values, and institutions we have cherished appears to be crumbling while we watch.

But we should not be deceived or disheartened. God is in fact the arch-enemy of chaos, the creator of order and goodness and the architect of all of history. God is in control.

We often misinterpret history as the record of mankind's accomplishments -- which it isn't -- rather than the unfolding of God's plan -- which it is. That plan has a clearly defined end: God will make everything right. In that day things will be what they seem.

Unlike any other business in the United States, sports must preserve an illusion of perfect innocence.

-- Author Lewis H. Lapham

**The forces of good and decency often seem
helpless before evil's power, but don't be fooled:
God is in control and will set things right.**

DAY 15

NEVER TOO LATE

Read Genesis 21:1-7.

"And [Sarah] added, 'Who would have said to Abraham that Sarah would nurse children? Yet I have borne him a son in his old age'" (v. 7).

Terrence Rencher was such an indifferent student during his undergraduate days at Texas that he didn't even graduate. His daughter changed all that.

Rencher came to Austin from the Bronx as one of coach Tom Penders' prize recruits in 1991. He was an instant smash on the basketball court, setting the Longhorn freshman scoring record with 37 points against Virginia Commonwealth in January 1992 (a mark subsequently matched by Kevin Durant). He was a four-year starter, finishing in 1995 as the school's all-time leading scorer, breaking the record Travis Mays had set in 1990.

Rencher's resounding success on the court, however, did not carry over into the classroom. He admitted to being an indifferent student. "I was the guy who was carefree for the most part," he said. "I didn't know the importance of academics." His school work got so bad that as a sophomore, he was suspended for two games because of academic problems.

So he didn't think too much of it when he began a pro career after failing to graduate from Texas. As the years went by, however, Rencher's circumstances and attitude changed. When he finished his pro career, he was a married man with a house in Austin and money in the bank. And a daughter in kindergarten. Rencher realized that when he spoke to his daughter about the value of education -- well, it wouldn't sound too good coming from him. "I can't be hypocritical about school. I have to show her through my actions," he said.

So in the spring of 2007, Rencher enrolled at Texas again. On Dec. 8, 2007, more than fifteen years after he began his first college course, Terrence Rencher walked across the stage and received his degree in education. He called it "a great day."

Getting that college degree. Getting married. Starting a new career. Though we may make all kinds of excuses, it's often never too late for life-changing decisions and milestones.

This is especially true in our faith life, which is based on God's promises. Abraham was 100 and Sarah was 90 when their first child was born. They were old folks even by the Bible's standards at the dawn of history. But God had promised them a child and just as God always does, he kept his promise no matter how unlikely it seemed.

God has made us all a promise of new life and hope through Jesus Christ. At any time in our lives – today even -- we can regret the things we have done wrong and the way we have lived, ask God in Jesus' name to forgive us for them, and discover a new way of living – forever.

It's never too late to change. God promised.

I always knew that I was going to get my degree.
-- Terrence Rencher on returning to school

It's never too late to change a life
by turning it over to Jesus.

SIZE MATTERS

Read Luke 19:1-10.

*"[Zacchaeus] wanted to see who Jesus was, but being a
short man he could not, because of the crowd. So he ran
ahead and climbed a sycamore-fig tree to see him" (vv.
3-4).*

Malcolm Kutner would be an All-American football player for
Texas, but he was so scrawny when he first showed up that he had
to beg the coaches to let him play.

When Longhorn football coaches first saw Kutner, they pointed
him toward the basketball court. "I had to beg to go out for football," he recalled. "I was a scrawny kid, a (basketball) center, even
though I wasn't built like a center."

Kutner did manage to talk his way onto the football field in
1938. He worked hard to bulk up his 6-foot-2 frame, and in 1941,
he and Chal Daniels became the first consensus All-Americas in
Texas football history. He played both ways at end. He is a member of the Longhorn Hall of Honor and was inducted into the
National Football Foundation Hall of Fame in 1974.

Kutner played in a day with no scholarships; he had to work for
his room and board. His first job was joining the other freshmen
in sweeping the floor of Gregory Gym; varsity players monitored
the broom wielders. He also sold "soda water" at basketball and
baseball games.

His last job was much more important, though Kutner didn't

realize it at the time. He was paid $40 a month by the athletic department to go through the state's major newspapers, find articles about high school football players, and put them in a big scrapbook. Thus did he lay the recruiting foundation for head football coach Dana X. Bible and his staff.

By the time he was a senior, this "tall, scrawny kid" who was too small to play football weighed 194 pounds. "I got by with speed and good hands," Kutner said about his All-American football career. And, by 1941, some size helped out.

Bigger is better! Such is one of the most powerful mantras of our time. We expand our football stadiums. We augment our body parts. Hey, make that a triple cheeseburger and a large order of fries! My company is bigger than your company. Even our church buildings must be bigger to be better. About the only exception to our all-consuming drive for bigness is our waistlines.

But size obviously didn't matter to Jesus. After all, salvation came to the house of an evil tax collector who was so short he had to climb a tree to catch a glimpse of Jesus. Zacchaeus indeed had a big bank account; he was a big man in town even if his own people scorned him. But none of that – including Zacchaeus' height – mattered; Zacchaeus received salvation because of his repentance, which revealed itself in a changed life.

The same is true for us today. What matters is the size of the heart devoted to our Lord.

It is not the size of a man but the size of his heart that matters.
-- Evander Holyfield

Size matters to Jesus, but only the size of the heart of the one who would follow Him.

DAY 17

CHEERS

Read Matthew 21:1-11.

*"The crowds that went ahead of him and those that
followed shouted" (v. 9).*

For today's Texas fans, the distinctive "Hook-'em-Horns" sign
is as synonymous with Longhorn athletics as Bevo and "The Eyes
of Texas." It wasn't always that way, though.

The 1955 season offered several indelible changes to Texas foot-
ball. The season included the introduction of night football and
"Big Bertha," the band's 500-lb. drum. The most lasting tradition,
however, came from a 19-year-old student cheerleader named
Harley Clark, Jr. Clark was so enthusiastic that he went to coach
Ed Price and volunteered to help the team's student managers.
He hauled equipment and lent a hand at every practice.

One of the stories about the genesis of the Longhorn symbol
relates that a friend of Clark's, fellow student Henry Pitts, was
playing around making animal shadows on his dorm wall. "He
extended the index and little fingers with the middle and ring
fingers tucked under the thumb" and thought that it resembled
a Longhorn. He passed on to Clark his suggestion that Texas
needed a hand sign similar to Texas A&M's "gig-em, thumbs-up
sign" and showed the cheerleader his creation.

Clark tried the Hook-'em-Horns sign on several students, who
invariably "though it was corny." Undeterred, Clark unveiled the
sign at a Friday night pep rally in Gregory Gym before about 4,000

students. "You could see the idea catch on," Clark said. "It swept around the horseshoe, and you could see the older fans doing it."

The sign was all over the place at the game the next day, but it didn't help as TCU blasted the Horns, who were on their way to a 5-5 season. "The sign was about all we had left," Clark said.

The sign obviously never went away, which surprised Clark. 'It's been very gratifying," he once said, "even though it never occurred to me that it would be the object of such great interest."

Chances are you go to work every day, do your job well, and then go home to your family. This country couldn't run without you; you're indispensable to the nation's efficiency. Even so, nobody cheers for you, waves pompoms in your face, or creates special hand signs to urge you on. Your name probably will never elicit a standing ovation when a PA announcer calls it.

It's just as well, since public opinion is notoriously fickle. Consider what happened to Jesus. When he entered Jerusalem, he was the object of raucous cheering and an impromptu parade. The crowd's adulation reached such a frenzy they tore branches off trees and threw their clothes on the ground.

Five days later the crowd shouted again, only this time they screamed for Jesus' execution.

So don't worry too much about not having your personal set of cheering fans. Remember that you do have one personal cheerleader who will never stop pulling for you: God.

Ours has far surpassed A&M's sign.

– Harley Clark, Jr.

**Just like the sports stars, you do have
a personal cheerleader: God.**

JUGGERNAUT

Read Revelation 20.

"Fire came down from heaven and devoured them. And the devil, who deceived them, was thrown into the lake of burning sulfur, where the beast and the false prophet had been thrown" (vv. 9b-10a).

How's this for a juggernaut that will certainly never be replicated in major college basketball? The Texas women once won 189 straight games against Southwest Conference opponents, an incredible streak that stretched across thirteen seasons.

Nobody took too much notice when the Texas women lost to Texas A&M 59-52 on Jan. 23, 1978. The program was in its fourth season, and back then the NCAA and the media ignored women's sports altogether. Jody Conradt was in her second season as the head coach. Her starters were Retha Swindell, Cathy Burns, Linda Andrews Waggoner, Kim Basinger, and Alisha Nelson.

On Nov. 29, 1977, the women and Temple Junior College played the first basketball game ever held in the new Special Events Center. In January of that season, the Texas women had their first-ever game programs. It would be the next season before they would have their first media guide.

As the Longhorns evolved into the biggest conference bully major college basketball has ever seen, however, that loss became significant. It was the last time the women would lose to an SWC foe until No. 25 Arkansas beat them on Feb. 23, 1990, a stretch of

189 games. Technically, the streak against actual conference foes was 130 -- still an unbelievable number -- since the old league didn't become the framework for women's basketball until 1983.

Clarissa Davis, Kamie Ethridge, Andrea Lloyd, Annette Smith, and Beverly Williams were All-Americas during the NCAA portion of the streak. Prior to the switch to the NCAA, Swindell and Waggoner played during the streak and were All-Americas.

Maybe your experience with a juggernaut involved a game against a team full of major college prospects, a league tennis match against a former college player, or your presentation for the project you knew didn't stand a chance. Whatever it was, you've been slam-dunked before.

Being part of a juggernaut is certainly more fun than being in the way of one. Just ask all those helpless 189 Texas opponents. Or consider the forces of evil aligned against God. At least the teams that took the court against the Texas women for all those years had some hope, however slim, that they might pull out a win. No such hope exists for those who oppose God.

That's because their fate is already spelled out in detail. It's in the book; we all know how the story ends. God's enemies may talk big and bluster now, but they will be trounced in the most decisive defeat of all time.

You sure want to be on the winning side in that one.

The people at the University of Texas are making a commitment to go first class and give the women whatever it takes to be the best.
                                        -- Philadelphia Inquirer *in 1977*

**The most lopsided victory in all of history is a
sure thing: God's ultimate triumph over evil.**

FAITHFUL LIVES

Read Hebrews 11:1-12.

"Faith is the substance of things hoped for, the evidence of things not seen" (v. 1 NKJV).

At Texas, Chris Hall preached what he practiced.

He practiced football. As a senior center in 2009, he was third-team All-America. As a sophomore in 2007, he started at least one game at all five positions on the offensive line, leading line coach Mac McWhorter to call him "the most versatile player I've had in 34 years."

But Chris Hall also practiced a way of life; he was and is a man of faith in Jesus Christ. At Texas he was quite literally a BMOC because of his size and his fame as a starter on a team that played for the national championship. But for Hall, BMOC meant "Big Man of Christ."

He was a licensed minister while he was at Texas. Football academic counselor Brian Davis said of Hall, "He's not a fake athlete who blesses the meal before the orgy commences. He's the most absolute, sincere true believer in faith and mankind."

In other words, Hall put that absolute faith into practice in his daily life. He was known to ask the Lord to forgive a driver who had pulled out in front of him in traffic rather than lapse into road rage. "I've never seen him without a smile on his face," said offensive coordinator Greg Davis. "With [Chris], the glass isn't half full. It's running over."

LONGHORNS

During the summer of 2006, Brian Davis was not having a very good day, particularly because he faced the unpleasant chore of ripping into three players for some quite unbecoming conduct. He stormed out of his office and was confronted by the trio of troublemakers, huddled in a circle, heads bowed as Hall led them in prayer. "I closed the door," Davis said, "went back into my office and said, 'God bless Chris Hall.'"

As it is with Chris Hall, your faith forms the heart and soul of what you are. Faith in people, things, ideologies, and concepts to a large extent determines how you spend your life. You believe in the Longhorns, in your family, in the basic goodness of Americans, in freedom and liberty, and in abiding by the law. These beliefs mold you and make you the person you are.

This is all great stuff, of course, that makes for decent human beings and productive lives. None of it, however, is as important as what you believe about Jesus. To have faith in Jesus is to believe his message of hope and salvation as recorded in the Bible. True faith in Jesus, however, has an additional component; it must also include a personal commitment to him. In other words, you don't just believe in Jesus; you live for him.

Faith in Jesus does more than shape your life; it determines your eternity.

All you really have, when all is said and done, are your friends, your family, and your faith.

-- *Mack Brown*

Your belief system is the foundation upon which you build a life; faith in Jesus is the foundation for your eternal life.

JUST PERFECT

Read Matthew 5:43-48.

"Be perfect, therefore, as your heavenly Father is perfect"
(v. 48).

On yet another afternoon when Cat Osterman was perfect, the best throw of the game probably was one her catcher made.

Osterman has been called "probably the most dominant athlete ever to play a sport for Texas." From 2002-2006 (with the exception of the year she took off in 2004 to win an Olympic Gold Medal), she won 136 games for the Horns. She finished her career in Austin with the lowest ERA in NCAA history (.05065) and the highest average of strikeouts per seven innings (14.34) in NCAA history. She was a four-time All-America and three-time national Player of the Year. Along the way, Osterman threw twenty no-hitters and ten perfect games.

She was closing in on one of those perfect games on May 21, 2005, against Mississippi State in an NCAA regional game. Mic-Kayla Padilla scored off an error in the third inning, and Amber Hall stroked an RBI single in the fourth to stake Osterman to a 2-0 lead. On the mound, Osterman rolled along; she struck out the first nine batters she faced and didn't need her outfielders, since none of them ever touched a live ball.

With one out in the seventh, Osterman notched yet another of her 17 strikeouts for the game, but the ball got away from catcher Megan Willis. "I thought I caught it, but I looked at my glove and it wasn't there," Willis said. "I panicked because you worry about running into the umpire or hitting the runner with the ball. But it all worked out."

Indeed it did as Willis threw a strike to first base to preserve the perfect game, Osterman's second straight no-hitter and third in her last four games.

Except perhaps for Cat Osterman quite frequently, nobody is perfect; we all make mistakes every day. We botch our personal relationships; at work we seek competence, not perfection. To insist upon personal or professional perfection in our lives is to establish an impossibly high standard that will eventually destroy us physically, emotionally, and mentally.

Yet that is exactly the standard God sets for us. Our love is to be perfect, never ceasing, never failing, never qualified – just the way God loves us. And Jesus didn't limit his command to only preachers and goody-two-shoes types. All of his disciples are to be perfect as they navigate their way through the world's ambiguous definition and understanding of love.

But that's impossible! Well, not necessarily, if to love perfectly is to serve God wholeheartedly and to follow Jesus with single-minded devotion. Anyhow, in his perfect love for us, God makes allowance for our imperfect love and the consequences of it in the perfection of Jesus.

I wasn't going to be the one to ruin it.
-- Megan Willis on a passed ball costing a perfect game

In his perfect love for us, God provides
a way for us to escape the consequences
of our imperfect love for him: Jesus.

FUTURE PERFECT

Read Matthew 6:25-34.

"Do not worry about tomorrow, for tomorrow will worry about itself" (v. 34).

By the time he was eight years old, Robert Brewer knew what the future held for him: He would be a quarterback for the University of Texas. The problem was that when the time came, nobody else saw that future.

When the 8-year-old Brewer met Texas coach Darrell Royal in a restaurant, Royal told him, "You've got good-size hands. You'd make a good quarterback." Brewer held onto that dream of a future as a Longhorn, but he turned out to be what he called a "pretty average" quarterback in high school. He nevertheless confidently told Texas head coach Fred Akers he was going to play quarterback for him. Akers saw a skinny kid nobody -- including Texas -- was recruiting.

Brewer walked on at Texas and went by Akers' office to ask him one question: "Can I have any kind of chance?" Akers responded, "If you are good enough, you will get a chance." That was enough to keep the future alive -- but just barely. Brewer languished on the bench deep into his junior season of 1981 when the 6-1 Longhorns ran into trouble against Houston. Two first-half interceptions led to two Cougar touchdowns and a 14-0 lead; to make it worse, starting quarterback Rick McIvor was injured trying to make a tackle on one of the picks.

Akers decided to give Brewer a try. Receiver Herkie Walls told Brewer, "You are not the No. 2 quarterback any more, so don't play like it." He didn't. He led Texas to two touchdowns and a 14-14 tie, the difference in the Horns ultimately earning the conference's bid to the Cotton Bowl where they upset third-ranked Alabama.

In 1982, Brewer continued to catch up to his future by quarterbacking the Horns to a 9-3 record, tossing what was then a school-record twelve touchdown passes.

We worry about many things, but nothing tops the frequency with which we fret about tomorrow. How would we live if I lost my job? How can we pay for our children's college? What will I do when my parents can't take care of themselves? What will the Longhorns do next season?

Amid our worries about the future, along comes Jesus to tell us, in effect, "Don't worry. Be happy." Well, that's all right for Jesus, but he never had a mortgage to pay, biopsy results to sweat out, or teenagers in the house to worry about.

In telling us how to approach tomorrow, though, Jesus understood a crucial aspect of the future: Your future is determined by how you live in the present. Particularly is this true in your spiritual life. God has carefully planned your eternal future to include unremitting glory, joy, and peace. It's called Heaven.

You must, however, claim that future in the present through faith in Jesus. And then – don't worry about it.

The future ain't what it used to be.

-- *Yogi Berra*

**You lay claim to a sure future
through a present faith in Jesus Christ.**

MEMORY LOSS

Read 1 Corinthians 11:17-29.

"[D]o this in remembrance of me" (v. 24).

One of Texas' legendary football players played on and even scored a touchdown after being knocked so silly he couldn't remember the plays and wound up losing his memory for a week.

Harrison Stafford arrived in Austin in 1929 and announced he wanted to play football. His first Texas uniform was a torn jersey and mismatched shoes. But freshman coach Shorty Alderson quickly made his excited way to head coach Clyde Littlefield and told him, "I found you the darndest football player you ever saw. He tore up a couple of dummies and hurt a couple of men."

Stafford introduced himself to the varsity in rather spectacular fashion. The star of the team was halfback Dexter Shelley, who refused to play with a helmet because he couldn't see when he wore it. At Stafford's first practice, he flattened Shelley, who, still lying on the ground dazed, said to Alderson, "I've been playing football for nine years, and that's the hardest I've ever been hit."

Stafford made his reputation as a ferocious blocking back and a sure tackler. As a senior in 1932, he was second-team All-America and was the MVP of the Southwest Conference. He was one of the first twelve people inducted into the Longhorn Hall of Honor and was elected to the College Football Hall of Fame in 1973. Stafford was a star hurdler for the track team and also participated in the sprint relays, the long jump, the shot put, and the javelin.

LONGHORNS

In the 1930 Oklahoma game, Stafford caused a fumble that set up a tying touchdown by Ernie Koy. Later, Stafford scored the touchdown that sealed the 17-7 win. He scored it without any recollection of doing so, having probably suffered a concussion making a tackle. "I don't remember anything of the game," he later said. His teammates had to tell him what to do on the plays, and he said he didn't get his memory back for a week or more.

Memory makes us who we are. Whether our memories are dreams or nightmares, they shape us and to a large extent determine both our actions and our reactions. Alzheimer's is so terrifying because it steals our memory from us, and in the process we lose ourselves. We disappear.

The greatest tragedy of our lives is that God remembers. In response to that memory, he condemns us for our sin. On the other hand, the greatest joy of our lives is that God remembers. In response to that memory, he came as Jesus to wash even the memory of our sins away.

Through memory, we encounter revival. At the Last Supper, Jesus instructed his disciples and us to remember. In sharing this unique meal with fellow believers and remembering Jesus and his actions, we meet Christ again, not just as a memory but as an actual living presence.

To remember is to keep our faith alive.

I had to put a schedule of my classes in my notebook and then check it and my watch to see where I was supposed to be.
-- Harrison Stafford on his memory loss after the Oklahoma game

**We remember Jesus,
and God will not remember our sins.**

FOR THE FUN OF IT

Read Nehemiah 8:1-12.

"Do not grieve, for the joy of the Lord is your strength"
(v. 10c).

Man, I can have some fun with this." So thought Quan Cosby as he gathered in a long UTEP field-goal try.

On Sept. 6, 2008, the Longhorns played the University of Texas at El Paso Miners for the first time since 1933 when UTEP was still known as the Texas College of Mines. The underdog Miners kicked a pair of early field goals for a 6-0 lead before Colt McCoy hit Cosby for a 16-yard touchdown near the end of the first quarter. The whole evening would be fun for the senior wide receiver; he caught eight passes for a career-high 154 yards.

Texas led only 14-6 when UTEP tried a 65-yard field goal. That's when Cosby saw his chance to have a little more fun. On long attempts, he went in as the return man. Defensive backs coach Duane Akina had Cosby well versed on the rules, including the one that allowed him to run a short attempt out of the end zone. But head coach Mack Brown had some stipulations on this particular return. Because of the rules, Texas would get the ball at the 48 if the kick were no good. "If you think you can go farther than that, go for it," Brown said.

The kick came down just short of the goal posts at the back of the end zone. The smart move may have been to take a knee, but Cosby caught the ball, looked up, and saw a whole lot of real estate in front of him. That's when he realized that this kick could be a whole lot of fun. He took off and wound up returning the kick 65 yards to the Miner 35. The Longhorns quickly scored, and the whole team went on to have a lot of fun in a 42-13 win.

Somewhere along the way, a very erroneous stereotype of the Christian lifestyle has emerged, that of a dour, sour-faced person always on the prowl to sniff out fun and frivolity and shut it down. "Somewhere, sometime, somebody's having fun – and it's got to stop!" Many understand this to be the mandate that governs the Christian life.

But even the Puritans, from whom that American stereotype largely comes, had parties, wore bright colors, and allowed their children to play games.

God's attitude toward fun is clearly illustrated by Nehemiah's instructions to the Israelites after Ezra had read them God's commandments. They broke out into tears because they had failed God, but Nehemiah instructed them not to cry but to eat, drink, and be merry instead. Go have fun, believers! Celebrate God's goodness and forgiveness!

This is still our mandate today because a life spent in an awareness of God's presence is all about celebrating, rejoicing, and enjoying God's countless gifts, especially salvation in Jesus Christ. To live for Jesus is to truly know the fun in living.

I don't count on the boy who waits till October, when it's cool and fun, then decides he wants to play.

-- Darrell Royal

What in God's wonderful Earth can be more fun that living for Jesus?

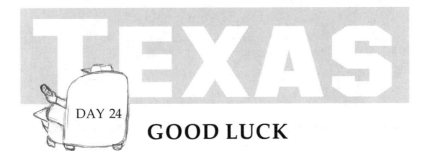

GOOD LUCK

Read Acts 1:15-25.

*"Then they prayed, 'Lord, you know everyone's heart.
Show us which of these two you have chosen.' . . . Then
they cast lots" (vv. 24, 25a).*

Because he felt lucky, the trainer helped the Longhorn baseball team to its third national title.

The 1975 College World Series was down to three teams, each with one loss: Texas, Arizona State, and South Carolina. The rules then called for the teams to draw for a bye. In the fifth inning of the 17-6 romp over South Carolina that would set up the drawing, trainer Spanky Stephens went to head coach Cliff Gustafson and said, "I feel lucky. I can draw the bye." Quite seriously, the coach replied, "Are you sure?" "Yeah, I'm sure," was the answer.

When the game ended, Gustafson said to Stephens, "Let's go," and they walked to home plate. As Stephens recalled it, "I picked up the envelope and opened it. . . . I turned it over and it said 'bye.'" Gustafson was already jumping up and down with joy; his Longhorns would play for the national championship.

The team rode around Omaha on a yellow school bus in those more austere days. On the ride back to the hotel after the win and the luck of the draw, Gustafson simply told his players, "All right, men, we've got one more to go."

South Carolina eliminated Arizona 4-1 with four runs in the ninth, setting up a one-game playoff for the national title. The

Horns scored a single run in the first and were never headed. Sophomore Mickey Reichenbach, the series MVP after hitting .455, slammed a two-run homer in the third. Junior Richard Wortham, who only months before had suffered a leg injury so serious he wondered if he would ever walk again, pitched a four-hit masterpiece, walking one and striking out nine.

The national champions won 5-1 to end the season 56-6. They weren't lucky; they were just hard-down good.

Ever think sometimes that other people have all the luck? Some guy wins a lottery while you can't get a raise of a few lousy bucks at work. The football takes a lucky bounce the other team's way and Texas loses a game. If you have any luck to speak of, it's bad.

To ascribe anything that happens in life to blind luck, however, is to believe that random chance controls everything, including you. But here's the truth: There is no such thing as luck, good or bad. Even when the apostles in effect flipped a coin to pick the new guy, they acknowledged that the lots merely revealed to them a decision God had already made.

It's true that we can't explain why some people skate merrily through life while others suffer in horrifying ways. We don't know why good things happen to bad people and vice versa. But none of it results from luck, unless you want to attribute that name to the force that does indeed control the universe; you know -- the one more commonly called God.

Luck is what happens when preparation meets opportunity.
-- Darrell Royal

**A force does exist that is in charge,
but it isn't luck; it's God.**

DOWNRIGHT CRAZY

Read Luke 13:31-35.

"Some Pharisees came to Jesus and said to him, 'Leave this place and go somewhere else. Herod wants to kill you.' He replied, 'Go tell that fox . . . I must keep going today and tomorrow and the next day'" (vv. 31-33).

The play call was so crazy that John Mackovic had made it only once in his twelve years as a college coach -- but now seemed like a good time to run it a second time.

The play was called Steelers Roll Left. The offense lined up in a tight goal-line formation, and the quarterback sprinted out with a pass-run option. Texas had often practiced the play, and Mackovic had used it occasionally in goal-line situations. But only once before had he called it on fourth down in his own territory. That had been almost a decade before at Illinois. "We didn't make it, and people called me crazy," he said.

But in the first-ever Big 12 championship game on Dec. 7, 1996, Mackovic made the call for a second time, knowing full well that he would be called crazy again since the Horns would lose the game if the play didn't work. The 7-4 Longhorns were unranked and were 20-point underdogs to the once-beaten Nebraska Corn-huskers, the defending national champions. Texas led 30-27 with 2:40 to play and faced fourth and inches on its own 28.

That's when Mackovic called the play, directing quarterback James Brown to run first after faking a handoff to Priest Holmes.

He was to pass only if he had nowhere to run to. But expecting a run, the Husker defense bit on the fake. As Brown headed for the first-down marker, he spotted sophomore tight end Derek Lewis wide open downfield. Brown lofted a strike to Lewis, who rumbled to the Nebraska 11. On the next play, Holmes scored.

Texas won 37-27 in a game that seized a firm place in Longhorn football lore. The Horns went down in history as the winners of the first-ever Big 12 title game.

"Calling that play took guts," said senior linebacker Tyson King. And a little craziness.

What some see as crazy often is shrewd instead. Like the time you went into business for yourself or when you decided to go back to school. Maybe it was when you fixed up that old house. Or when you bought that new company's stock.

You know a good thing when you see it but are also shrewd enough to spot something that's downright crazy. Jesus was that way too. He knew that his entering Jerusalem was in complete defiance of all apparent reason and logic since a whole bunch of folks who wanted to kill him were waiting for him there.

Nevertheless, he went because he also knew that when the great drama had played out he would defeat not only his personal enemies but the most fearsome enemy of all: death itself.

It was, after all, a shrewd move that provided the way to your salvation.

If you are going to be a champion, you have to go for it.
-- John Mackovic on why he made his crazy call

**It's so good it sounds crazy -- but it's not: through
faith in Jesus, you can have eternal life with God.**

ATTITUDE CHECK

Read 1 Thessalonians 5:12-22.

"Give thanks in all circumstances, for this is God's will for you in Christ Jesus" (v. 18).

Once upon a time not too awfully long ago, the attitude was pretty widespread that it wasn't cool to play basketball for Texas. T.J. Ford changed all that.

One of the primary reasons for Texas' decision to throw in with the formation of the Big 12 Conference in 1996 was a desire for a higher profile in basketball. Under Tom Penders, the program had averaged better than 20 wins a season from 1988-98. After a losing 1997-98 campaign, Rick Barnes took over and found himself trying to stem a veritable exodus: "Recruits were leaving Texas and starring at schools throughout the nation."

Everything changed in 2001 when Barnes signed Ford, a 6'0" guard who was the state's most highly recruited player. "Everybody in the world wanted T.J.," said Barnes. "It was a real coup for us to get him. He made it cool to come to Texas."

Perhaps that was in part because of the cool way Ford played the game, relishing setting up baskets for his teammates rather than scoring himself. "He would dish and glide on the hardwood, and he glided right into the hearts of the [Texas] fans."

Ford became the first freshman in history to top the nation in assists as he led the Horns to a 22-12 record and the Sweet Sixteen in 2001-02. He then led the team in scoring and assists as a sophomore and into the Final Four for the first time since 1947. He became the first Longhorn player ever to win the Naismith and Wooden awards as the top player in college ball.

His importance to Texas basketball went beyond just his on-court performance. With "his contagious smile and his ability to interact with people," he was a great ambassador for the school. "He made it all right to come to Texas," Barnes said.

How's your attitude? You can fuss because your house is not as big as some, because a coworker talks too much, or because you have to take a handful of pills every day. Or you can appreciate your home for providing warmth and shelter, the co-worker for the lively conversation, and the medicine for keeping you reasonably healthy.

Whether life is endured or enjoyed depends largely on your attitude. An attitude of thankfulness to God offers you the best chance to get the most out of your life because living in gratitude means you choose joy in your life no matter what your circumstances. This world does not exist to satisfy you, so chances are it will not. True contentment and joy are found in a deep, abiding relationship with God, and the proper way to approach God is not with haughtiness or anger but with gratitude for all he has given you.

[T.J. Ford has] done more for Texas basketball than any player before him. He changed the attitude of Texas basketball.

-- Rick Barnes

**Your attitude goes a long way
toward determining the quality of your life
and your relationship with God.**

AS A RULE

Read Luke 5:27-32.

"Why do you eat and drink with tax collectors and 'sinners'?" (v. 30b)

A rule change that Darrell Royal opposed was instrumental in launching the Texas football program's return to glory.

When the Longhorns met Oklahoma in 1958, Royal was in his second year in Austin. The Sooners had dominated the series in recent years, winning six straight times. "Texas has to develop a football tradition," Royal said. "It had one once but lost it." Rediscovering that football tradition at Texas more than anything else meant putting a stop to "that bloodletting up at Dallas."

Prior to the 1958 season, the NCAA made a major change in the game when it approved the two-point conversion after touchdowns. As a dyed-in-the-wool purist, Royal opposed the change. But then when the Horns scored the first touchdown in the 1958 Oklahoma game, Royal surprised everyone: He went for two.

The decision was no surprise for his team, though. Royal had decided on Friday to go for two if the Horns scored first. "We felt in this ball game one touchdown wouldn't hold up," Royal explained.

The play was a straight hand-off to fullback Don Allen. When Royal saw the Sooners' defensive formation, he knew the play would work. "I knew that their tackle and end could not get there fast enough to stop the play. If our guard could block their linebacker, it was a walk-in." The guard, H.G. Anderson, "stuck his hat in the Oklahoma player's belly so that only the ear flaps were showing," said offensive line coach Jim Pittman. Allen did indeed walk in for an 8-0 lead.

As the game unfolded, Royal's use of that new rule was the difference. Texas won 15-14, the first NCAA game to be decided by a two-point conversion. Not coincidentally, the Horns won 12-of-13 games in the series starting in '58. Texas was back.

You live by rules others have set up. Some lender determined the interest rate on your mortgage. You work hours and shifts somebody else established. Someone else decided what day your garbage gets picked up and what school district your house is in.

Jesus encountered societal rules also, including a strict set of religious edicts that dictated what company he should keep, what people, in other words, were fit for him to socialize with, talk to, or share a meal with. Jesus ignored the rules, choosing love instead of mindless obedience and demonstrating his disdain for society's rules by mingling with the outcasts, the lowlifes, the poor, and the misfits.

You, too, have to choose when you find yourself in the presence of someone whom society deems undesirable. Will you choose the rules or love? Are you willing to be a rebel for love — as Jesus was for you?

We were shooting for the win.
-- Darrell Royal on why he went for two

Society's rules dictate who is acceptable
and who is not, but love in the name of Jesus
knows no such distinctions.

GOD'S CONQUERORS

Read John 16:19-33.

"In this world you will have trouble. But take heart! I have overcome the world" (v. 33b).

For a football team, overcoming the opposition is tough enough, but the 1918 Texas squad had a pair of unprecedented and especially tough foes to battle: a world war and a flu pandemic.

The flu that ravaged the world in 1918 claimed more than 50 million lives. As October and the football season began, the *Austin Statesman* declared the 100 flu cases at Camp Mabry to be "of a mild type and no apprehension is felt."

Two days later, though, a soldier died in Fort Worth, and by Oct. 7 the University of Texas was shut down. "The student barracks became influenza wards." To prevent the spread of the dreaded disease, an Austin city ordinance prevented public gatherings, which meant the cancellation of football games, including the Texas-Oklahoma game.

But the flu wasn't the only obstacle the Horns had to overcome. World War I was raging in Europe, and "war planners were turning college campuses into de facto military outposts." That war effort included the University. Coach Bill Juneau's football team could practice only after both school and military obligations were completed. Some of the most promising players left for officer training school. Team captain Charlie "Fats" Conley tried to enlist but was turned down because of his weight. Still,

LONGHORNS

he went home to his family farm and waited to be drafted.

The team beat TCU 19-0 before the flu temporarily shut the school down. The depleted squad played a few makeshift games, closed to the public, against the Penn Radio School team from South Austin and a squad from Ream Flying Field. But then the school reopened, an armistice was declared, and the Horns won games over Rice, SMU, and A&M, finishing the unorthodox season 9-0. As a reminder of how implacable the flu was, guard Joe Spence fell ill after the A&M game and died.

We often hear inspiring stories of people who triumph by overcoming especially daunting obstacles. Those barriers may be physical or mental disabilities or great personal tragedies or injustice. When we hear of them, we may well respond with a little prayer of thanksgiving that life has been kinder to us.

But all people of faith, no matter how drastic the obstacles they face, must ultimately overcome the same opponent: the Satan-infested world. Some do have it tougher than others, but we all must fight daily to remain confident and optimistic.

To merely survive from day to day is to give up by surrendering our trust in God's involvement in our daily life. To overcome, however, is to stand up to the world and fight its temptations that would erode the armor of our faith in Jesus Christ.

Today is a day for you to overcome by remaining faithful. The very hosts of Heaven wait to hail the conquering hero.

All semblance of regular college life was gone.

-- UT yearbook in 1918

Life's difficulties provide us a chance to experience the true joy of victory in Jesus.

GOD'S HOUSE

Read 2 Samuel 7:1-7.

"I have not dwelt in a house from the day I brought the Israelites up out of Egypt to this day. I have been moving from place to place with a tent as my dwelling" (v. 6).

From a marriage proposal to a record-setting night to an all-star volleyball career -- three generations of the Howden family have known a strong attachment to Gregory Gym.

In 1949, a Texas student named Raymond Smith walked up to the ticket window in Gregory where his girlfriend, Bebe Suiter, worked. Young Raymond flashed a diamond ring at her and asked, "Do they sell these here?" They were married in 1950.

They had a daughter named Debi who attended Texas and took a part-time job in that same ticket office. She met a basketball player named Lynn Howden in that same gym. Lynn liked the cozy little place that seated about 7,000. "The fans were right on top of you," he recalled. "We didn't mind diving for loose balls. You might land in a pretty girl's lap." On Dec. 1, 1970, in the opening game of the season, the 6-foot-7 Lynn pulled down 24 rebounds against FSU, a school record that still stands.

Debi saw Lynn shooting in the gym one day, so she decided to give the friendship a little tweaking. She walked over and asked, "You want me to show you how to do this?" Debi admitted the move was "kind of flirtatious." It worked.

Their daughter, Bethany, stretched the attachment to Gregory

LONGHORNS

Gym across three generations of the family when she joined the Longhorn volleyball team in 2001. The middle blocker and outside hitter was a freshman All-America and a three-time All-Big 12 selection.

Lynn constantly reminded his daughter that he had played in the building before the 1997 renovation when conditions had been much tougher. The building had no air conditioning, for instance. One thing about the renovation that upset Debi was the conversion of the old ticket office into a men's rest room.

Buildings play a pivotal roles in our lives, and we often become quite attached to them as the Howden family has to old Gregory Gym. A favorite restaurant. A football stadium or basketball gymnasium. The house you grew up in.

But what about a church? How important is that particular facility to you? Is it just the place where you were married? Where you were baptized? Is it nothing more than a house of memories or where you go to out of habit to placate the spouse?

Or is it the place where you regularly go to meet God? After all, that's what a church building really is: a place built expressly for God. It's God house. Long ago, the only place God could visit his people was in a lousy tent. Nowadays, churches serve as the site where God's people meet both to worship and to encounter him.

In a church alive with a true love of God, he is always there. Whether you find him or not depends on how hard you look -- and whether you're searching for him with all your heart.

I love Gregory Gym. I still get a thrill going there.

-- Bebe Smith

When you visit God in his house, do you find him?

A SURE THING

Read Romans 8:28-30.

"We know that in all things God works for the good of those who love him, who have been called according to his purpose" (v. 28).

At the outset, the offense that produced two national championships "and a 30-game winning streak that rocked the college football world" wasn't a sure thing. Fans booed it and the players didn't like it.

In the spring of 1968, Darrell Royal wanted to find a way to get fullbacks Steve Worster and Ted Koy on the field at the same time. The solution came from offensive backfield coach Emory Bellard, who had "piddled around in his yard with his son" and had come up with an offense that featured three backs behind the quarterback. Quarterback Eddie Phillips recalled that in the fall of 1968, Bellard introduced the basic principles of the novel option offense to him over breakfast, using salt and pepper shakers.

The players weren't too sure about this newfangled formation. "We all had a lot of doubts," said quarterback James Street. "We really didn't think it could work." "I was very skeptical myself because it eliminated my position," said former wingback Randy Peschel, who moved to split end.

The new offense, which was eventually dubbed the Wishbone, debuted on Sept. 21 in the season opener against Houston. The original backfield comprised quarterback Bill Bradley, fullback

Worster, and halfbacks Koy and Chris Gilbert. The unveiling was somewhat less than smashing, a 20-20 tie. Late in the game, Royal elected to run out the clock rather than throw a pass. The sellout crowd booed lustily. "I can't say I disagreed with them," Gilbert said.

Royal and Bellard tinkered with the offense, though, and the Longhorns broke six conference team offense records that season alone. The suspect offense turned college football upside down.

Football games aren't played on paper. That is, you attend a Texas game expecting the Longhorns to win, but you don't know for sure. If you did, why bother to go? Any football game worth watching carries with it an element of uncertainty.

Life doesn't get played on paper either, which means that living, too, comes laden with uncertainty. You never know what's going to happen tomorrow or even an hour from now. Oh, sure, you think you know. For instance, right now you may be certain that you'll be at work Monday morning or that you'll have a job next month. Life's uncertainties, though, can intervene at any time and disrupt your nice, pat expectations.

Ironically, while you can't know for sure about this afternoon, you can know for certain about forever. Eternity is a sure thing because it's in God's hands. Your unwavering faith and God's sure promises lock in a certain future for you.

It's kind of scary when you're told you're not going to block some guy [the defensive end].
-- Quarterback James Street's reservations about the Wishbone

Life is unpredictable, tomorrow is uncertain; only eternity is a sure thing because God controls it.

DAY 31

CONFIDENCE MAN

Read Micah 7:5-7.

"As for me, I will look to the Lord, I will wait for the God of my salvation" (v. 7 NRSV).

Longhorn head coach Fred Akers was not interested in attempting a really long field goal. His kicker was so confident, though, that he talked Akers into it and then went out and delivered the points that were the difference in a stirring upset of Arkansas.

The 1983 Horns went 11-0 thanks largely to their "suffocating defense and pressure-resistant kicker." That kicker was freshman Jeff Ward, who that season set a school record for accuracy that still stands: He hit 15 of 16 field goal attempts, a percentage of .938. In 1985, Ward set a school record by making thirteen straight field goals. (Phil Dawson subsequently broke Ward's record with fifteen straight in 1996-97.)

Ward was apparently immune to pressure because he was so confident. He was confident enough about his kicking abilities to reject scholarship offers to play wide receiver. "I knew I would be an average wide receiver," he said. "I knew I could be a good field goal kicker if that's all I did."

Perhaps at no time was Ward's confidence more in evidence than in the Arkansas game of 1985. "No one thought we could win," Ward admitted. But the defense held Arkansas to 13 points, and Ward kicked field goals of 34, 33, 49, 55, and 34 yards. He had to talk Akers into the 55-yarder. "Fred was saying we need the field position, and I said, no, we need the points," Ward recalled. When Ward's holder, Danny Akers, the coach's son, endorsed the kick, the head Horn relented and sent the kicking unit onto the field. Ward put up the points and UT won 15-13.

The confident Ward led the team in scoring all four seasons. In the 32 wins Ward was involved in, his field goals made the difference in thirteen of them.

You need confidence in all areas of your life. You're confident the company you work for will pay you on time, or you wouldn't go to work. You turn the ignition confident that your car will start. When you flip a switch, you expect the light to come on.

Confidence in other people and in things is often misplaced, though. Companies go broke; car batteries die; light bulbs burn out. Even the people you love the most sometimes let you down.

So where can you place your trust with absolute confidence you won't be betrayed? In the promises of God.

Such confidence is easy, of course, when everything's going your way, but what about when you cry as Micah did, "What misery is mine!" As Micah declares, that's when your confidence in God must be its strongest. That's when you wait for the Lord confident that God will not fail you, that he will never let you down.

When it gets right down to the wood-chopping, the key to winning is confidence.

-- *Darrell Royal*

People, things, and organizations
will let you down; only God can be trusted
absolutely and confidently.

STRANGE BUT TRUE

Read Isaiah 9:2-7.

"The zeal of the Lord Almighty will accomplish this" (v. 7).

Strange but true: The woman most responsible for the construction of a women's gymnasium on campus was also responsible for the elimination of women's intercollegiate basketball at Texas.

UT's first women's intercollegiate basketball game was played in 1906. The sport expanded slowly with only a few sporadic intercollegiate games in those early years; it remained "mostly an intramural, interclass affair." A new era arrived in 1921 when Anna Hiss was named director of women's PE. For almost 40 years, this "visionary in directing physical education" "was among the most prominent women on campus." She started a degree program for PE majors and was ambitious and innovative in her dedication to women's physical education and intramural sports.

Strangely enough, Hiss was dead set against intercollegiate athletics for women, especially basketball. "She abhored [*sic*] the male model, governed -- as she saw it -- by money and skewed educational values." She totally disapproved of pampered, elite athletes who received fawning attention and excessive school resources.

Thus, at Texas, women's basketball changed drastically once Hiss took over. Games against outside schools stopped, and the

LONGHORNS

sport became nothing more than intramural and interclass play. Hiss even headed up a national attack on basketball, which she characterized as "unfeminine and dangerous" and said was "too physically and emotionally strenuous for women."

Her crowning achievement was the construction in 1931 of the $400,000 Women's Gymnasium, which was renamed for her in 1972 after her death. It included three playing courts, but they were all undersized to discourage basketball competition.

Some things in life are so strange their existence can't really be explained. How else can we account for the sport of curling, tofu, that people go to bars hoping to meet the "right" person, the proliferation of tattoos, and the behavior of teenagers?

And how strange is God's plan to save us? Think a minute about what God did. He could have come roaring down, destroying and blasting everyone whose sinfulness offended him, which, of course, is pretty much all of us. Then he could have brushed off his hands, nodded the divine head, and left a scorched planet in his wake. All in a day's work.

Instead, God came up with a totally novel plan: He would save the world by becoming a human being, letting himself be humiliated, tortured, and killed, and thus establishing a kingdom of justice and righteousness that will last forever.

It's a strange way to save the world – but it's true.

It may sound strange, but many champions are made champions by setbacks.

-- Olympic champion Bob Richards

**It's strange but true: God allowed himself
to be killed on a cross to save the world.**

DAY 33

ALIVE AGAIN

Read Matthew 28:1-10.

"He is not here; he has risen, just as he said. Come and see the place where he lay" (v. 6).

A 5-4 season doesn't sound like much for Longhorn football. That record, though, included the moment in 1939 that pretty much single-handedly resurrected the dormant UT program.

From 1893 through 1932, the Texas Longhorns never had a losing season in football. Then came a 4-5-2 record in 1933 followed by a 7-2-1 season in 1934. After that, though, the program tumbled into the tank with four straight losing seasons, capped by the awful 1-8 season of 1938 that included a 42-6 loss to Arkansas.

In 1939, coach Dana X. Bible was in the third year of his effort to turn the herd around, but it was a hard road. "Things had been down for so long," recalled Bill Sansing, a student at the time whom Bible would hire as Texas' first sports information director. "There was a loser mentality."

The Horns were 2-1 when the favored Razorbacks strode into Memorial Stadium. Sophomore halfback Jack Crain, who was All-Southwest Conference in 1939 and '41, put the Horns on the scoreboard with an 82-yard punt return, but Arkansas led 13-7 with thirty seconds to play.

As disheartened Texas fans streamed toward the exits, Bible instructed the band director to play "The Eyes of Texas," called a time out, and had his players stand and listen to the song. Duly inspired, quarterback Johnny Gill made up a play in the huddle. He switched positions with Crain, and fullback R.B. Patrick took the snap. Patrick flipped a screen pass to Crain, who went 67 yards to tie the game. Ecstatic Longhorn fans stormed the field; police needed several minutes to clear it for the extra point. Crain's kick was good and Texas won 14-13.

"That play and that victory changed our outlook," Bible said. Sansing asserted that "before that, everything was down. After that, everything was on the way up." The resurrected Texas football program would not have another losing season until 1954.

We often speak figuratively of resurrected careers in sports. We use resurrection language when a team comes from way behind to win a game or turns a season or even a program around with a big win.

While so-called resurrections do occur in the New Testament, they are actually only resuscitations since they result only in the postponement of death. One in particular stands alone, however.

When Jesus miraculously walked out of that tomb on the first Easter morning, he threw off not only his burial cloths but death itself. On that day, God created something new: the resurrection life that one day will be the only one.

That's because resurrection is a fact of life for the followers of Jesus. When Christ left that tomb behind, he also left death behind for all who believe that he is indeed the savior of the world.

It was the renaissance of Texas football.
-- Bill Sansing on the 1939 win over Arkansas

Jesus' resurrection forever ended death's hold
on life; life has won.

DRY RUN

Read John 4:1-15.

"Everyone who drinks this water will be thirsty again, but whoever drinks the water I give him will never thirst. Indeed, the water I give him will become in him a spring of water welling up to eternal life" (vv. 13-14).

The Longhorns were oh-for-life against Kansas in its digs, but the drought came to a resounding end in one of the biggest games of the 2010-11 season.

The UT men had never won at Allen Field House in Lawrence, losing seven straight times over the years. They weren't alone; KU had won 69 consecutive home games when the Horns sauntered confidently into their house on Jan. 22. The table was clearly set for Texas to be Victim No. 70. The Horns weren't exactly cannon fodder; they were 15-3 and ranked No. 10 in the nation. It's just that the Jayhawks were 18-0 and ranked No. 2.

And the home team came out red hot, making seven of its first ten shots and grabbing an 18-3 lead with 5:18 gone in the game. Turn out the lights; let the Jayhawk fans begin serenading the beaten Horns with their chant, "Rock Chalk Jayhawk."

But the Horns lived and died all that season with their defense. They went into the Kansas game having held their eighteen opponents to only 37 percent shooting. While UT head coach Rick Barnes wasn't too excited about the 15-point Kansas lead, he also wasn't too disturbed by it. He didn't even call a time out to try to slow Kansas down.

As it turned out, the Texas defense simply demolished the UK offense. "They're an inside-out team with their offense," said sophomore Jordan Hamilton, who scored 17 points. "We took that away from them." That meant the Texas defense turned the Jayhawk players into a bunch of outside shooters, and they didn't do very well from out there.

When the game was over, so was the drought on the road at Kansas. The Horns won going away 74-63.

You can walk across that river you boated on in the spring. The city's put all neighborhoods on water restriction. That beautiful lawn you fertilized and seeded will turn a sickly, pale green and may lapse all the way to brown. Somebody wrote "Wash Me" on the rear window of your truck.

The sun bakes everything, including the concrete. The earth itself seems exhausted, just barely hanging on. It's a drought.

It's the way a soul that shuts God out looks.

God instilled thirst in us to warn us of our body's need for physical water. He also gave us a spiritual thirst that can be quenched only by his presence in our lives. Without God, we are like tumbleweeds, dried out and windblown, offering the illusion of life where there is only death.

Living water – water of life – is readily available in Jesus. We may drink our fill, and thus we slake our thirst and end our soul's drought – forever.

Time to start another streak.
-- Resigned KU fan on the way to his car after the Texas win

Our soul thirsts for God's refreshing presence.

| DAY 35 |

PRECIOUS MEMORIES

Read 1 Thessalonians 3:6-13.

"Timothy . . . has brought good news about your faith and love. He has told us that you always have pleasant memories of us" (v. 6).

The Longhorns once remembered a fallen teammate by intentionally not making an extra point.

Mack Brown's recruiting class of 1999 was voted the nation's No. 1 bunch. They won 40 games while they were in Austin. Quarterback Chris Simms, defensive end Cory Redding, and defensive back Nathan Vasher moved on to the pros.

Among the stellar recruits of the class was defensive lineman Cole Pittman. He played in every game in 1999 and 2000, moving into a starter's slot for three games as a sophomore. On Feb. 26, 2001, he died in a one-vehicle accident while he was returning to Austin from his home in Shreveport.

His teammates dedicated the 2001 season to him, and his locker with his No. 44 jersey became a shrine. The season's second game, against North Carolina, was chosen to honor him. Before the game, his family was presented with a framed No. 44 jersey and other mementos of Pittman's truncated time as a Longhorn.

On their way to an 11-2 record that included a win over Washington in the Holiday Bowl, the Horns crushed the Tar Heels. Sophomore running back Brett Robin scored with 36 seconds left to play, his touchdown upping the score to 44-14. The players at once realized the significance of the 44 points. Thus, instead of lining up to kick the extra point, the Horns snapped the ball for a play. Quarterback Major Applewhite took the snap and knelt down to keep the scoreboard total at 44 in Pittman's honor.

While you probably don't enjoy dwelling on such things, your whole life will one day be only a memory as was Cole Pittman's to his teammates. With that knowledge in hand, you can control much about your inevitable funeral. You can, for instance, select a funeral home, purchase a cemetery plot, pick out your casket or a tasteful urn, designate those who will deliver your eulogy, and make other less important decisions about your send-off.

What you cannot control about your death, however, is how you will be remembered and whether your demise leaves a gaping hole in the lives of those with whom you shared your life or a pothole that's quickly paved over. What determines whether those nice words someone will say about you are heartfelt truth or just pleasant fabrications to cover up the reality of your life? What determines whether the tears that fall at your death result from heartfelt grief or a sinus infection?

Love does. Just as Paul wrote, the love you give away during your life decides whether or not memories of you will be precious and pleasant.

I don't want my children to remember me as a professional football player. I want them to remember me as a man of God.
— Reggie White

How you will be remembered after you die is largely determined by how much and how deeply you love others now.

SMART MOVE

Read 1 Kings 4:29-34; 11:1-6.

"[Solomon] was wiser than any other man. . . . As Solomon grew old, his wives turned his heart after other gods, and his heart was not fully devoted to the Lord his God" (vv. 4:31, 11:4).

One of the smartest moves Darrell Royal ever made had to do with smarts first and football second.

Royal arrived in Austin in the spring of 1957 to rehabilitate a program that had been 1-9 in 1956 and discovered to his dismay that fifteen of his would-be players were academically ineligible. "We had enough players," Royal said. "We didn't need a recruiter as much as we [needed] an academic counselor."

So Royal made a smart move that today is a routine part of college athletics. He hired Lan Hewlett as his players' "brain coach." Hewlett, a former Texas student who had played in the marching band, had a master's degree in bacteriology and was a former major in the Army. He thus became the first academic counselor in college football history. "I guess you would have to say that Darrell invented me," Hewlett said about his position.

"The day of the dumb athlete, if it ever existed, is definitely over," Hewlett asserted. He backed up his claim with records that showed the grade point average of the university's athletes to be higher than that of the overall student body.

The youthful Royal had openly, if somewhat ideally, criticized the stereotype of the dumb jock, insisting that big-time athletics and high academic standards were not incompatible. His brainstorm -- the "brain coach" -- proved him correct. By the fall of '58, only three football players were academically ineligible. "It was the best move I ever made," Royal said.

It was certainly a smart one.

Remember that time you wrecked the car when you spilled hot coffee on your lap? That cold morning you fell out of the boat? The time you gave your honey a tool box for her birthday?

Formal education notwithstanding, we all make some dumb moves sometime because time spent in a classroom is not an accurate gauge of common sense or of how we will respond under pressure. Folks impressed with their own smarts often grace us with erudite pronouncements that we intuitively recognize as flawed, unworkable, or simply wrong.

A good example is the oft-repeated dictum that great intelligence and scholarship are not compatible with faith in God. That is, the more we know, the less we believe. But any incompatibility occurs only because we begin to trust in our own wisdom rather than the wisdom of God. We forget, as Solomon did, that God is the ultimate source of all our knowledge and wisdom and that even our ability to learn is a gift from God.

Not smart at all.

[Having academic counseling] is like religion. Everyone should have some of it.

-- Lan Hewlett

Being truly smart means trusting in God's wisdom rather than only in our own knowledge.

A FAST START

Read Acts 2:40-47.

"Everyone was filled with awe. . . . [They] ate together with glad and sincere hearts, praising God and enjoying the favor of all the people" (vv. 43a, 46b, 47a).

Like other head coaches, Mack Brown preached the importance of a fast start, especially in a game against a favored opponent. In the Alamo Bowl of 2012, though, the Horns got off to such a slow start that the head Horn scrapped the game plan at halftime.

UT's start in the game of Dec. 29 against 15th-ranked Oregon State was rather kindly described by one writer as "dismal." The Longhorn offense wasn't offensive at all, scratching out 23 yards in 15 plays in the first quarter. Texas didn't have a first down until the opening play of the second quarter -- and that came on an OSU penalty.

While the Longhorn offense struggled in its attempt to establish a running game, the Beavers went about the business of establishing a ten-point lead. At halftime, Brown told his offensive assistants to forget everything they had planned on doing.

The Horns switched to a no-huddle offense, and sophomore quarterback David Ash and the offense put some points on the board. OSU took advantage of its fast start, though, to take a 27-17 lead into the fourth quarter. That didn't look too encouraging for UT, since the team hadn't overcome a deficit of more than seven points all season.

But midway through the last quarter, Ash found freshman running back Johnathan Gray for a 15-yard TD toss. The defense rose up with defensive ends Alex Okafor and Cedric Reed sacking the OSU quarterback on third-and-13 to force a punt.

With 2:24 to play, Ash, who completed his last seven passes, lofted a 36-yard touchdown pass to wide receiver and Olympian Marquise Goodwin, voted the game's most outstanding offensive player. When Okafar led another defensive stand, the slow-starting but fast-finishing Longhorns had a 31-27 bowl win.

Fast starts are crucial for more than football games and races. Any time we begin something new, we want to get out of the gate quickly and jump ahead of the pack and stay there. We seek to build up momentum from a fast start and keep rolling.

This is true for our faith life also. For a time after we accepted Christ as our savior, we were on fire with a zeal that wouldn't let us rest, much like the early Christians described in Acts. All too many Christians, however, let that blaze die down until only old ashes remain. We become lukewarm pew sitters.

The Christian life shouldn't be that way. Just because we were tepid yesterday doesn't mean we can't be boiling today. Every day we can turn to God for a spiritual tune-up that will put a new spark in our faith life; with a little tending that spark can soon become a raging fire. Today could be the day our faith life gets off to a fast start – again.

Hey, forget it. Let's go.
   -- Mack Brown at halftime on the Alamo Bowl game plan

**Every day offers us yet another chance
to get off to a fast start for Jesus.**

KEEPING THE PEACE

Read Hebrews 12:14-17.

"Make every effort to live in peace with all men and to be holy" (v. 14).

Before he was a football and basketball player for Texas, Ed "Shipwreck" Kelley would get his kicks by clearing out the riffraff in waterfront bars. Thus, mouthing off to Kelley during a game was not a particularly good idea. One lineman from North Carolina made that mistake -- with predictable results.

The 1948 Longhorn football team went 7-3-1, finished second in the Southwest Conference, and upset favored Georgia 41-28 in the Orange Bowl. (See Devotion No. 80.) They demolished LSU 33-0 in the opener but ran into a buzz saw the following week against a North Carolina team that would go undefeated and finish third in the nation. "They beat us like a drum," declared UT back Tom Landry. "It was the worst licking we took all the time I was at Texas," recalled end Ralph "Peppy" Blount.

Tackle "Shipwreck" Kelley didn't take too kindly to the drubbing. He had received his unforgettable nickname from trainer Frank Medina, who had been duly inspired by the physical way in which Kelley cleared out the lanes in a basketball game much as he had a waterfront bar in his past. He "would foul out in four minutes," Blount asserted.

As the score mounted and the afternoon grew longer for the Horns, the guard across from Kelley rubbed it in. "This little

LONGHORNS

waterplug guard would tell Ed, 'How do you like it today, you big [so and so],'" Blount remembered. Finally, Kelley had enough. He "cocked that forearm and hit that kid under the chin," said Blount. "He raised him a good foot off the ground. I mean, he's out cold. Not even his toe is wiggling. I thought Kelley had killed him."

The kid survived the blow, and Longhorn coach Blair Cherry made Shipwreck apologize to the Tar Heels. On the flight home, though, when Blount asked Kelley if he had really apologized, Kelley replied, "Yes, but I wanted to tell all them, I hope they broke all their legs and never walked again."

Perhaps you've never been in a brawl to match that of Shipwreck Kelley on the waterfront. But maybe you retaliated when you got an elbow in a pickup basketball game. Or maybe you and your spouse or your teenager get into it occasionally, shouting and saying cruel things. Or road rage may be a part of your life.

While we do seem to live in a more belligerent, confrontational society than ever before, fighting is still not the solution to a problem. Rather, it only escalates the whole confrontation, leaving wounded pride, intransigence, and simmering hatred in its wake. Actively seeking and making peace is the way to a solution that lasts and heals broken relationships and aching hearts.

While peacemaking is admittedly not as easy as fighting, it is much more courageous and a lot less painful. It is also exactly what Jesus would do.

I went to a fight last night and a hockey game broke out.
-- Comedian Rodney Dangerfield

Making peace instead of fighting takes courage
and strength; it's also what Jesus would do.

STORY TIME

Read Luke 8:26-39.

"'Return home and tell how much God has done for you.'
So the man went away and told all over town how much
Jesus had done for him" (v. 39).

From a massive, coordinated toilet flush to the pen of a fallen Longhorn legend, the University of Texas has its stories to tell.

The expansion and renovation of Texas Memorial Stadium in the 1990s included an extensive reworking of the facility's sewer system, which at the time consisted of the original plumbing of 1924. Adding more rest rooms didn't help if the flush didn't flow, so sewer lines had to be added. To test out the new plumbing, all athletic department employees were dispatched to the stadium rest rooms one day and, on cue, executed a massive simultaneous flush. Let history record that the flush flowed.

Abe Lemons, UT men's basketball coach from 1976-82, didn't like the bizarre rule that banned dunking in pre-game warmups. When Miss. State was hit with a technical foul for dunking prior to a 1976 game, Lemons ordered his star, Jim Krivacs, a 90-percent free-throw shooter, to shoot the charity shot facing away from the basket. The crowd loved it, but Texas lost the game in overtime; the one point would have made a difference in the outcome. Asked about it, the undaunted Lemons replied, "Shoot, he almost made it."

Jack Chevigny coached the football team from 1934-36, leading

LONGHORNS

the Horns to the memorable upset of Notre Dame in 1934. (See Devotion No. 59.) As a memento of the legendary win, his team gave him a gold pen and pencil set engraved "To Jack Chevigny, an old Notre Damer who beat Notre Dame." Chevigny was a Marine officer in World War II and was killed at Iwo Jima. At the Japanese surrender ceremony aboard the battleship *Missouri* to end the war, an American officer noticed a gold pen being used. He asked to see it and read the inscription; it was Chevigny's pen.

Like those involved with University of Texas athletics, you, too, have a story to tell; it's the story of your life and it's unique. No one else among the billions of people on this planet has a life story that matches yours.

Part of that story is your encounter with Jesus. It's the most important chapter of all, but all too often believers in Jesus Christ don't tell it. Otherwise brave and daring Christian men and women who wouldn't think twice of skydiving or white-water rafting often quail when they are faced with the prospect of speaking about Jesus to someone else. It's the dreaded "W" word: witness. "I just don't know what to say," we sputter.

But witnessing is nothing but telling your story. No one can refute it; no one can claim it isn't true. You don't get into some great theological debate for which you're ill prepared. You just tell the beautiful, awesome story of Jesus and you.

To succeed in your sport or your life, you have to go out and write your own story.

-- *Motivational-Quotes-for-Athletes.com*

We all have a story to tell, but the most important part of all is the chapter where we meet Jesus.

DAY 40

THE HOMEPLACE

Read Joshua 24:14-27.

*"Choose for yourselves this day whom you will serve. . . .
But as for me and my household, we will serve the Lord"*
(v. 15).

From 1928-74, the Texas baseball team had a unique and powerful home-field advantage: Billy Goat Hill.

The original site for Longhorn baseball was Clark Field. In 1928, a new Clark Field opened, a facility still considered to be "one of the most unique and charismatic baseball fields in America."

Clark Field (II) was nestled into the natural hills and landscape of the area, described by one writer as "the most lovely and harmonious baseball field in the United States." That harmony with the surroundings resulted in Billy Goat Hill, the field's most distinctive feature.

Billy Goat Hill was a 12- to 30-foot limestone cliff that ran from left-center to right center field. Naturally, this made playing the outfield -- particularly center field -- quite an adventure, especially for the unwary visitor.

The cliff received its name because it was accessible only via a goat path in left-center. This didn't keep some particularly adept Longhorn center fielders from figuring out how to scale the thing and thus limit towering fly balls to doubles rather than home runs. Accounts of the era assert that Clarence Pfeil and Pete Layden, teammates in 1939 and 1940, were among the best at using Billy

LONGHORNS

Goat Hill to their advantage. Some Texas center fielders adopted the novel strategy of playing atop the hill to keep the ball in front of them. The other outfielders positioned themselves far off the lines to help cover the full outfield.

Visitors always had trouble figuring out how to play the hill. One adventuresome A&M center fielder tried to play atop it but then couldn't figure out how to get down the thing. The game was held up for several minutes while the embarrassed Aggie made his way to the ground via the safe goat path.

Your home, too, is a unique place. You enter it to find love, joy, and security. It's the place where your heart feels warmest, your laughter comes easiest, and your life is its richest. It is the center of and the reason for everything you do and everything you are.

How can a home be such a place?

If it is a home where grace is spoken before every meal, it is such a place. If it is a home where the Bible is read, studied, and discussed by the whole family gathered together, it is such a place. If it is a home that serves as a jumping-off point for the whole family to go to church, not just on Sunday morning and not just occasionally, but regularly, it is such a place. If it is a home where the name of God is spoken with reverence and awe and not with disrespect and indifference, it is such a place.

In other words, a house becomes a true home when God is part of the family.

Sure, the home field is an advantage, but so is having a lot of talent.
-- Dan Marino

A home is full when all the family members –
including God -- are present.

WINNER'S CIRCLE

Read 1 John 5:1-12.

"Who is it that overcomes the world? Only he who believes that Jesus is the Son of God" (v. 5).

On Nov. 21, 2009, what Longhorn fans already knew became official: Colt McCoy is a winner.

The quarterback's fellow seniors joined him in a celebratory dogpile that night after the Horns had annihilated Kansas 51-20 to remain undefeated,. The win clinched a berth in the conference title game and kept the team's national title hopes alive. What made the victory special enough to require a dogpile was that it was the 43rd of McCoy's storied college career, which made him the winningest quarterback in college football history.

Playing his last game in his home stadium, McCoy had one of his best nights. "I don't think he could have scripted it any better," said head coach Mack Brown. McCoy left the game with 5:22 to play having completed 32 of 41 passes for 396 yards and four touchdowns. He rushed for 44 more yards and even quick-kicked once, pinning the helpless Jayhawks down at their own 12. During the night, he became only the fifth player in college football history to account for more than 14,000 yards in a career.

As had been true during the years the duo had played together, Jordan Shipley was McCoy's favorite target. He caught 10 passes for 108 yards, including a 38-yard touchdown, and broke the UT record for most receiving yards in a season.

McCoy and the crowd didn't want the special night to get over. When the game ended, he shot off Smokey the cannon and, egged on by the band, took a lick or two at Big Bertha. The last player off the field, McCoy had to be ushered off by an associate athletic director. Even then, he "skipped and bounced through the tunnel, slapping a few high-fives along the way."

Colt McCoy and his Texas Longhorn teammates of 2009 were -- more than anything else -- winners.

Life itself, not just athletic events, is a competition. You go up against all the other job or college applicants. You compete with others for a date. Sibling rivalry is real; just ask your brother or your sister.

Inherent in any competition or any situation in which you strive to win is the involvement of an antagonist. You always have an opponent to overcome, even if it's an inanimate video game, a golf course, or even yourself.

Nobody wants to be numbered among life's losers. We recognize them when we see them, and maybe mutter a prayer that says something like, "There but for the grace of God go I."

But one adversary will defeat us: Death will claim us all. We can turn the tables on this foe, though; we can defeat the grave. A victory is possible, however, only through faith in Jesus Christ. With Jesus, we have hope beyond death because we have life.

With Jesus, we win. For all of eternity.

What is important to me is winning.

-- Colt McCoy

Death is the ultimate opponent;
Jesus is the ultimate victor.

LESSON LEARNED

Read Psalm 143.

"Teach me to do your will, for you are my God" (v. 10).

The Texas coaches were so intent on teaching their lesson that they rolled around on the ground to do it. The following Saturday, the lessons paid off with a clutch play against Arkansas.

The Horns opened the 2004 football season with a 65-0 blowout of North Texas, a game in which Texas did little wrong. Nevertheless, the coaches spotted something they considered important: Three times the Horns had put the ball on the ground.

So at practice Mack Brown gathered his charges around him to teach them a vital lesson as they prepared for Arkansas. "If somebody throws you a ball, put it away," he said. He then tossed a ball to assistant head coach Dick Tomey, who hugged the ball securely to his body. He tossed it back to Brown, who did the same.

Then the coaches went one step further. "And if you are walking across campus with a teammate, and somebody drops the ball, get on it," Brown barked. He then rolled the ball to Tomey, who dropped to the ground and curled into a fetal position with the ball secured next to his body. He then rolled it back to Brown, who did the same and rolled the ball to defensive tackles coach Mike Tolleson, who hit the ground and covered the ball.

The UT coaches were quite willing to get down and dirty to teach a lesson because they had noticed on game tapes that the Arkansas quarterback sometimes didn't secure the football. A fumble recovery, thus, might be crucial in the game's outcome.

So there they were on Saturday. With less than three minutes to play, Texas led 22-20, but the Hogs were well within field-goal range. They decided to run one more play, a pass. The quarterback took the snap, and 2005 All-American Michael Huff led a defensive charge. Junior tackle Larry Dibbles stripped the ball free. Two Arkansas players reached for it, but safety Michael Griffin did just as he had been shown in practice, falling on the ball and tucking it safely away. Texas had a 22-20 win.

Learning about anything in life requires a combination of education and experience. Education is the accumulation of facts that we call knowledge; experience is the acquisition of wisdom and discernment, which add understanding to our knowledge.

The most difficult way to learn is through trial and error: dive in blindly and mess up. The best way to learn is through example coupled with instructions: Someone has gone ahead to show you the way and has written down all the information you need to follow.

In teaching us the way to live godly lives, God chose the latter method. He set down in his book the habits, actions, and attitudes that make for a way of life in accordance with his wishes. He also sent us Jesus to explain and to illustrate.

God teaches us not only how to exist but how to live. We just need to be attentive students.

It was textbook training, exactly as he had been coached.
— Bill Little on Michael Griffin's fumble recovery

To learn from Jesus is to learn what life is all
about and how God means for us to live it.

OF GENTLE MEN

Read John 2:13-22.

"He made a whip out of cords, and drove all from the temple area . . .; he scattered the coins of the money changers and overturned their tables" (v. 15).

With his team playing on the biggest stage in the country, Texas head basketball coach Jack Gray was determined to behave with dignity, as a gentleman should. But, hey, a bad call is a bad call.

Gray was UT's first basketball All-America. Only two seasons after his playing days ended, he was named the Texas head coach in 1937; he was 25. In 1939, in an effort to give his program some national exposure, Gray took the Horns over the Christmas holidays to what was then the Promised Land of American sports -- Madison Square Garden in New York City -- to play Manhattan as part of a doubleheader. In this hallowed sports temple, coaches and players alike were expected to conduct themselves decorously at all times. On Dec. 26, 1939, Gray led his team into the Garden, promising himself that he would behave like the gentleman the venue required he be.

The crowd was the largest Texas had ever played before, and Gray was indeed a perfect gentleman as the game unfolded -- at least until his team suffered what he believed to be a particularly egregious call. Upset, Gray grabbed the nearest object he could find, a basketball, and slammed it to the floor as hard as he could. Immediately, he realized he had broken his promise. He refused to watch the ball rise toward the ceiling, looking instead to his team manager, Bill Sansing. "Has it come down yet?" he asked. "No, sir," Sansing replied. "But it's stopped going up."

The technical foul didn't hurt much; Texas won 54-32. On that day, though, Gray gave Sansing a new assignment to ensure he would behave like a gentleman during all games: "Sit by me, with your finger in my belt, and don't let me get up."

A calm, caring manner and a soft voice are often mistaken for weakness, and gentle men are frequently misunderstood by those who fail to appreciate their inner strength. But Jack Gray's athletic and coaching career and Jesus' rampage through the Jerusalem temple illustrate the perils of underestimating a determined gentleman.

A gentleman treats other people kindly, respectfully, and justly, and conducts himself ethically in all situations. A gentleman doesn't lack resolve or backbone. Instead, he determines to live in a way that is exceedingly difficult in our selfish, me-first society; he lives the lifestyle God desires for us all.

Included in that mode of living is the understanding that the best way to have a request honored is to make it civilly, with a smile. God works that way too. He could bully you and boss you around; you couldn't stop him. But instead, he gently requests your attention and politely waits for the courtesy of a reply.

Play to win, observe the rules, and act like a gentleman.
-- Basketball coach and author (and friend of Jack Gray) Clair Bee

God is a gentleman, soliciting your attention
politely and then patiently waiting for you
to give him the courtesy of a reply.

BEST FRIENDS

Read Ecclesiastes 4:9-12.

"If one falls down, his friend can help him up. But pity the man who falls and has no one to help him up!" (v. 10)

The 1976 football season was hard on Coach Darrell Royal, but it cemented his friendship with one of UT's greatest players ever.

Despite the presence of the great Earl Campbell in the backfield, the Horns were only 5-5-1 in a season that included a loss to North Texas State. The media crucified Royal, criticizing his ability to make decisions and openly wondering if he were too old to be coaching anymore and if he were out of touch with the contemporary player. With twenty winning seasons, 167 wins against 47 defeats, 11 Southwest Conference champions, and three national titles behind him at Texas, Royal stepped down.

In the locker room after the season-ending 29-12 win over the Arkansas Razorbacks, Royal told his players of his decision. Campbell, a junior, sat on a folding chair in the back of the room and listened to his "mentor, friend, and beloved coach" speak of the changing times and how tough it was for him to leave his players. Royal later recalled that Campbell was the only player who stayed for his entire retirement announcement.

Royal's decision devastated Campbell. As he left the stadium that evening with a heavy heart, he passed by two men who said good-bye by hugging each other and saying, "I love you." Campbell had never before witnessed such an open display of affection between two men. Thus prompted he sought Royal out, told his coach what he had just seen and said, "This touched me 'cause I didn't know what I was gonna say to you tonight in the event I saw you. Anyway, I just want you to know that no matter what happens, I'll always love you."

Royal ever afterward described Campbell as "a loyal, caring friend."

Lend him your car or some money. Provide tea, sympathy, and comfort when she's down. Talk him out of a bad decision such as attending Texas A&M. What wouldn't you do for a good friend?

We are wired for friendship. Our psyche drives us to seek both the superficial company of others that casual acquaintance provides and the more meaningful intimacy that true friendship furnishes. We are perhaps at our noblest when we selflessly help a friend.

So if we wouldn't think of turning our back on our friends, why would we not be the truest, most faithful friend of all by sharing with them the gospel of Jesus Christ? Without hesitating, we give a friend a ride, but we know someone for years and don't do what we can to save her from eternal damnation. Apparently, we are quite willing to spend all of eternity separated from our friends.

What kind of lousy friend is that?

When Earl Campbell takes someone as a friend, there's nothing he wouldn't do for them.

-- Darrell Royal

**A true friend introduces a friend
to his friend Jesus.**

YOU NEVER KNOW

Read Exodus 3:1-12.

"But Moses said to God, 'Who am I, that I should go to Pharaoh and bring the Israelites out of Egypt?' And God said, 'I will be with you'" (vv. 11-12a).

You never know what young men are capable of when they put on a Longhorn football uniform. For instance, a walk-on made two plays that "would alter the course of Texas football history."

"We were walk-ons." So declared Tom Campbell even though his twin brother and he technically had football scholarships to Texas. But that was in 1965 in the days of unlimited scholarships. Head coach Darrell Royal told his chief assistant, Mike Campbell, that his sons could have the last two scholarships and could stay as long as they wanted to.

In a stark contrast to all of the hoopla surrounding recruiting today, Daddy Campbell simply walked into the boys' room while they were studying and told them they were playing football for Texas. Tom figured they were "destined to hold up the blocking dummies so the real players could practice."

But you never know.

As it turned out, Tom Campbell was a starting linebacker as a junior and a starting defensive back as a senior in 1969. Most Longhorn fans at least know about the 44-yard pass from James Street to tight end Randy Peschel late in the fourth quarter that led to the decisive touchdown in the 15-14 win over No.-2 Arkansas in the "Game of the Century" in 1969. But it takes a true fan to know that a Tom Campbell interception at the Longhorn 21 sealed the game for Texas as Arkansas moved into field-goal range.

Longhorn fans may also vividly recall that in the 1970 Cotton Bowl, Street's fourth-down pass to Cotton Speyrer set up Billy Dale's winning touchdown that clinched Texas' national title. But how many fans know that it was Campbell who picked off Joe Theismann's final pass and allowed Texas to escape 21-17?

You never know what you can do until – like Tom Campbell -- you want to bad enough and get the chance or until – like Moses -- you have to. Serving in the military, maybe even in combat, for instance. Standing by a friend while everyone else unjustly excoriates her. Undergoing lengthy medical treatment and managing a smile through it all. You never know what life will demand of you.

It's that way too in your relationship with God. As Moses discovered, you never know where or when God will call you or what God will ask of you. You do know that God expects you to be faithful and willing to trust him even when he calls you to tasks that daunt and dismay you.

You can respond faithfully to whatever God calls you to do for him. That's because, though you never know what lies ahead, you do know that God will both lead you and provide all you need.

There's one word to describe baseball: You never know.
– Yogi Berra

You never know what God will ask you to do,
but you always know he will provide everything
you need to do it.

WHO, ME?

Read Judges 6:11-23.

*"'But Lord,' Gideon asked, 'how can I save Israel? My
clan is the weakest in Manasseh, and I am the least in my
family'" (v. 15).*

Texas won the 1982 Cotton Bowl on a touchdown scored by a
player who couldn't believe his number had been called.

The fifth-ranked Horns were underdogs to the third-ranked
Alabama Crimson Tide, and as the afternoon wore on, they looked
like it. After three quarters, quarterback Robert Brewer had been
sacked seven times, and the vaunted wishbone offense had come
no closer to scoring than a missed 50-yard field goal. Alabama
went up 10-0 with a field goal with 12:27 to play.

But the offense finally got untracked, moving to a first down at
the Tide 30. On third down, Brewer went the distance on a quarterback draw, a play Texas had not run since 1980.

After an Alabama punt, Brewer and the offense moved to the
Tide 8 in ten plays. During the drive, Brewer hit tight end Lawrence Sampleton with a pair of completions for 37 and 19 yards.
The quarterback draw had certainly been surprising enough, but
what Brewer called now was downright shocking: Play 24.

Play 24 was a simple, quick fullback dive over the right guard.
The fullback was Terry Orr, whose role in the wishbone offense
was clearly defined: He was a blocker for the team's flashy tail-
backs. When Orr heard the call, his eyes widened with disbelief.

"I was surprised," he said. "I was just waiting to hear who I was supposed to block."

Orr got the ball and promptly went the wrong way -- on purpose. He saw that left guard Joe Shearin had flattened his man and went behind that block into the end zone. With 2:05 to play, Texas was finally ahead 14-10. The Horns gave up a meaningless safety and won 14-12.

You probably know exactly how Terry Orr felt; you've experienced your own moment of surprise with a "who, me?" feeling that probably wasn't as exciting as his was. That time the teacher called on you when you hadn't done a lick of homework. Or the night the hypnotist pulled you out of a room full of folks to be his guinea pig. You've had the wide-eyed look and the turmoil in your midsection when you were suddenly singled out and found yourself in a situation you neither sought nor were prepared for.

You may feel exactly as Gideon did about being called to serve God in some way. You quail at the very notion of being audacious enough to teach Sunday school to a group of adults, coordinate prayer club at a local high school, or lead a small group study in your home. Who, me? Hey, who's worthy enough to do anything like that?

The truth is that nobody is – but that doesn't seem to matter to God. And it's his opinion, not yours, that counts.

Your brain commands your body to 'Run forward! Bend! Scoop up the ball! Peg it to the infield!' Then your body says, 'Who, me?'
-- Joe DiMaggio

You're right in that no one is worthy to serve God,
but the problem is that doesn't matter to God.

SOMETHING NEW

Read Colossians 3:1-17.

"[S]ince you have taken off your old self with its practices and have put on the new self, which is being renewed in knowledge in the image of its Creator" (vv. 9-10).

The new team in town held its first practice in the fall of 1995, and every one of the players showed up -- all four of them.

Their just-as-new head coach, Connie Clark, dubbed them the "Fab Four." They were the first four players to receive a scholarship to play softball for the University of Texas: Nikki Cockrell, Katie Penders, Ashley Hutchison, and Kim Lair.

The four moved around campus everywhere together, their friends invariably noting the shortage of warm bodies and asking, "Where's your team?" "They'd kid us -- 'They don't have softball here,'" said Penders, a freshman second baseman whose uncle, Tom, coached a little basketball on campus at the time.

Cockrell, a sophomore shortstop who transferred from Texas A&M, had a keen sense of the history they were making. "It's unbelievable," she said. "You get to set your own records. It's something special. We'll be able to get it started, and 20 years later we can look back down the road and see what we've accomplished."

Before the fall was over, though, the Fab Four did have some teammates as sixteen walk-ons joined them in October. That first team played a club schedule and then began NCAA play in the Big 12 a year later.

LONGHORNS

The new team in town didn't have a home it could call its own at first. While a spiffy new stadium was being constructed, the games of the first season were played at the East Austin Youth Complex field. The first UT game was played on Feb. 15, 1996, a day Cockrell called "a unique situation . . . that will go down in history."

By the third season, that new team was indeed making history, recording a 49-16 record, a top-10 national ranking, and the first-ever trip to the College World Series.

New things in our lives often have a life-changing effect. A new spouse. A new baby. A new job. A new college team. Even something as mundane as a new television set or lawn mower jolts us with change.

While new experiences, new people, and new toys may make our lives new, they can't make new lives for us. Inside, where it counts – down in the deepest recesses of our soul – we're still the same, no matter how desperately we may wish to change.

An inner restlessness drives us to seek escape from a life that is a monotonous routine. Such a mundane existence just isn't good enough for someone who is a child of God; it can't even be called living. We want more out of life; something's got to change.

The only hope for a new life lies in becoming a brand new man or woman. And that is possible only through Jesus Christ, he who can make all things new again.

[Other students] thought it was an imaginary team.
-- Fab Four member Katie Penders on Texas' new softball team

A brand new you with the promise
of a life worth living is waiting in Jesus Christ.

TOLD YOU SO

Read Matthew 24:15-31.

"See, I have told you ahead of time" (v. 25).

Vince Young could well have said, "I told you so," since the closing minutes of one of Texas' greatest games ever unfolded exactly as he said they would.

On Sept. 10, 2005, Texas took on Ohio State in the biggest non-conference game of the collegiate regular season. The Horns were ranked No. 2, Ohio State No. 4, but the homestanding Buckeyes had won 36 straight non-conference games and were one-point favorites.

The Horns promptly jumped out to an early 10-0 lead -- and then fell apart. Three turnovers helped propel Ohio State into a 19-13 lead. The teams swapped field goals in the third quarter to make it a 22-16 game. When the Buckeyes' offense cranked up a drive in the fourth quarter, some folks started turning out the lights on the Horns' party.

Not Young. He was with his offensive mates on the sideline, exhorting them and telling them exactly what was going to happen. "We've been through this," he said. "Defense is going to get us the ball, and we'll take it play by play." Sure enough, just as Young had told his guys, the defense held. Ohio State missed a 50-yard field goal try.

The Longhorns got the ball with five minutes left to play and 67 yards of grass to navigate with an offense that had generated only six points in its previous nine possessions. Just as Young had said, the offense took it play by play -- six of them, in fact. The sixth one was a 24-yard pass to wideout Limas Sweed, who made a leaping backward catch in double coverage in the end zone for his first-ever collegiate touchdown reception.

That came with 2:37 left. With 19 seconds on the clock, a safety from middle linebacker Aaron Harris put the final 25-22 score on the board. All Vince Young could really say was, "I told you so."

Unless it's a Longhorn, don't you just hate it in when somebody says, "I told you so"? That means the other person was right and you were wrong; that other person has spoken the truth. You could have listened to that know-it-all in the first place, but then you would have lost the chance yourself to crow, "I told you so."

In our pluralistic age and society, many view truth as relative, meaning absolute truth does not exist. All belief systems have equal value and merit. But this is a ghastly, dangerous fallacy because it ignores the truth that God proclaimed in the presence and words of Jesus.

In speaking the truth, Jesus told everybody exactly what he was going to do: come back and take his faithful followers with him. Those who don't listen or who don't believe will be left behind with those four awful words, "I told you so," ringing in their ears and wringing their souls.

All the kids that watched TV said nobody gave us any chance and you can't win here.
-- Mack Brown, engaging in a little 'I told you so' after the Ohio St. win

Jesus matter-of-factly told us what he has planned:
He will return to gather all the faithful to himself.

THE LEADER

Read Matthew 16:18-23.

"You are Peter, and on this rock I will build my church,
and the gates of Hades will not overcome it" (v. 18).

Bill Bradley walked around campus with tears in his eyes, figuring his days as a football player at Texas were over. But he decided not to give up and to become a team leader.

"Bill was one of the best athletes I've ever seen," said teammate Jim Helms. "He could play quarterback, wide receiver, defensive back, and he could punt." In 1966, Bradley was the first sophomore ever to start at quarterback for a Royal-coached team. In the third game of the season, he suffered cartilage damage in his knee that required surgery at year's end. He was so banged up in 1967 that, as he put, "I can remember playing where there was hardly an open spot on the right side of my body I was so taped up."

Royal switched to the wishbone offense in 1968, and the new formation was a disaster for Bradley. In the second game, Royal benched him and inserted James Street with the admonition, "You can't do any worse."

When Royal told Bradley that he was being moved to split end, the demoted quarterback "took a long walk all the way around campus with tears in my eyes, figuring the end was pretty close." But, Bradley noted, "My folks didn't bring me up to quit. . . . I decided I was going to become a leader."

Bradley did step up and become the fiery leader of his team.

LONGHORNS

Late in the season against Rice, he flattened a defender at the line of scrimmage, thereby unintentionally inventing the Texas bump-and-run. Defensive head coach Mike Campbell was so impressed that he talked Royal into making a defensive back out of Bradley. Despite having only a few games left in Austin, he became a star and went on to an All-Pro career as a defensive back.

Bill Bradley's leadership and talent helped lead the Horns to a 9-1-1 season and a 38-13 romp over Tennessee in the Cotton Bowl.

Every aspect of life that involves people – every organization, every group, every project, every team -- must have a leader. If goals are to be reached, somebody must take charge.

Even the early Christian church was no different. Jesus knew this, so he designated the leader in Simon Peter, who was such an unlikely choice to assume such an awesome, world-changing responsibility that Jesus soon after rebuked him as "Satan."

Author John MacArthur described Simon as "ambivalent, vacillating, impulsive, unsubmissive." Not much of a leader. Yet, Peter became, according to MacArthur, "the greatest preacher among the apostles" and the "dominant figure" in the church's birth.

The implication for your own life is both obvious and unsettling. You may think you lack the attributes necessary to make a good leader for Christ. But consider Simon Peter, an ordinary man who allowed Christ to rule his life and became the foundation upon which the Christian church was built.

I was still a captain and I'd show 'em what I was made of.
      -- Bill Bradley on his decision to become a team leader

**God's leaders are men and women
who allow Jesus to lead them.**

TRICK PLAYS

Read Acts 19:11-20.

"The evil spirit answered them, 'Jesus I know, and I know about Paul, but who are you?'" (v. 15)

Sarah Lancaster became a two-sport athlete at Texas because of a trick shot.

From 2007-10, Lancaster was a standout on the Texas women's tennis team. A four-time letter winner, she had a career record of 89-38 in singles, and was virtually unbeatable in the Big 12, rolling up a 40-1 record against conference opponents. ESPN named her to its Academic All-District Team in 2010.

As Lancaster's senior season wound down in 2010, her coach, Patty Fendick-McCain, kept urging her to try out for the basketball team. Under NCAA rules, an athlete has five years of eligibility if one year is spent in a different sport. Thus, Lancaster was eligible to play basketball for a year.

The senior treated the idea like the joke she thought it was. She had given up basketball to concentrate on tennis, figuring she wasn't good enough to play for the Longhorns. But Fendick-McCain knew what a good athlete Lancaster was and had seen her entertain her fellow tennis players with her trick shots when rain derailed practice. One day, Lancaster dribbled toward the basket, wrapped the ball around her waist and under her left leg, and casually flipped it through the hoop in one fluid motion.

A teammate videoed the trick shot, and Fendick-McCain forwarded it to women's basketball coach Gail Goestenkors. When the veteran coach saw the tape, she knew Lancaster could play and approached her about joining the team.

In 2010-11, the 5-9 guard saw action in almost half of Texas' basketball games and averaged about seven minutes of playing time. Lancaster made an immediate impression on her new coach by recording the fastest time in the mile run Goestenkors had ever seen in her nineteen seasons of college coaching. "She's a winner," the coach declared about her two-sport athlete.

And it all started with a trick play.

Scam artists are everywhere — and they love trick plays. For instance, an e-mail encourages you to send money to some foreign country to get rich. Or a loud television ad offers a miracle pill to help you lose weight without diet or exercise.

You've been around; you check things out before deciding. The same approach is necessary with spiritual matters, too, because false religions and bogus Christian denominations abound. The key is what any group does with Jesus. Is he the son of God, the ruler of the universe, and the only way to salvation? If not, then what the group espouses is something other than the true Word of God.

The good news about Jesus does indeed sound too good to be true. But the only catch is that there is no catch. No trick -- just the truth.

All the tennis girls thought it was the coolest thing ever.
-- Sarah Lancaster on her trick shot

God's promises through Jesus sound too good to be true, but the only catch is that there is no catch.

DAY 51

JUST IMAGINE

Read Revelation 1:4-18.

"His face was like the sun shining in all its brilliance. When I saw him, I fell at his feet as though dead" (vv. 16b-17a).

Before he made his first career start at middle linebacker for UT, Aaron Humphrey imagined making an interception -- which only goes to show that Humphrey doesn't have nearly enough imagination.

Humphrey made his reputation at Texas as a defensive end. As a senior in 1999, he led the Big 12 in sacks for the second straight season. He was the team's MVP and the Defensive Player of the Year for a squad that reached the Big 12 Championship game. He started as an outside linebacker his freshman season, and in the 1997 season-opener against Rutgers, he made his first-ever start at middle linebacker.

Part of his preparation for the game involved letting his imagination run wild. He quite naturally imagined himself making run-stuffing tackles and forcing fumbles. He even "imagined the unimaginable." "I visualized myself picking off a screen pass," he said, which was a stretch since he didn't have a single career interception and the coaches had frankly admitted some concerns about his pass defense.

Well, obviously, they never imagined that Humphrey would do what he did in the game on Sept. 6, 1997. The Longhorns routed

LONGHORNS

Rutgers 48-14. Ricky Williams had 19 carries for 155 yards that included touchdown runs of 74, 1, and 12 yards. Kicker Phil Dawson launched field goals of 52 and 54 yards, the latter a career long.

And Humphrey? He had a game that even he could never have imagined. He intercepted three passes.

We are blessed (or cursed) with generally active imaginations. We can, for instance, quite often imagine what someone or some place looks like from a description. We probably have in our minds an image of what Jesus the man looked like.

Some things, however, are beyond our imagining until we experience them or see them in person. Prejudice. The birth of our child. An October Saturday afternoon in Memorial Stadium. Falling in love. Time in prison.

And add to that list the glorified Jesus. When Jesus ascended to Heaven, he assumed his rightful place in glory right there with God the Father, another unimaginable sight. In so doing, Jesus, the gentle man who drew children close to him and wept over the death of a friend, achieved a radiant splendor and glory the likes of which we can't really imagine despite John's inspired attempt to describe the scene for us.

Imagine this: One day we will see the glorified Jesus face to face. What we can't imagine is the depth of the joy that meeting will bring us.

That was something I never could have imagined.
-- Aaron Humphrey on his three interceptions

The glorified Jesus is unimaginable
as is the joy we will experience
when we come into his presence.

DAY 52

SUPERSTITION

Read 1 Samuel 28:3-20.

"Saul then said to his attendants, 'Find me a woman who is a medium, so I may go and inquire of her'" (v. 7).

Convinced they were the victim of a hex, Texas students once consulted and then followed the advice of a local fortune teller to gain a win over Texas A&M.

Under coach Dana X. Bible, the 1941 Horns beat Colorado, LSU, Oklahoma, Arkansas, Rice, and SMU to move into AP's top spot for the first time in school history. *Life Magazine* made the team its cover story for the Nov. 17 issue just before the Baylor game. After the game, some fans grumbled about a cover jinx because the Bears tied Texas 7-7. The real reason for the upset, however, was the loss of four UT players to injuries suffered against SMU. Texas fell to No. 2 and then tumbled further with a last-minute loss to TCU.

Next up was the Thanksgiving Day game against the Aggies of Texas A&M at Kyle Field. The boys from College Station were unbeaten, ranked No. 2 in the country, and had already won the Southwest Conference title. Moreover, many folks believed that the Aggies' home field held a jinx for the Longhorns.

Texas had not won a game at Kyle Field since 1923. Seeking help wherever they could find it, some students consulted Madam Augusta Hipple, an Austin fortune teller. While she couldn't read the future, she certainly knew quite a bit about motivation. She instructed the students to burn red candles the week of the game to hex the Aggies. "They needed something to show the team they were behind them," she said.

Red candles showed up everywhere: along the Drag, in sorority and fraternity houses, in the lounges of residence halls, and in the windows of neighborhoods throughout town. The inevitable result was a uniting of the football team and its fans. Texas won 23-0 and wound up No. 4 in the country.

Black cats are right pretty. A medium is a steak. A key chain with a rabbit's foot wasn't too lucky for the rabbit. And what in the world is a blarney stone? About as superstitious as you get is to say "God bless you" when somebody sneezes.

You look indulgently upon good-luck charms, red candles in the windows, tarot cards, astrology, palm readers, and the like; they're really just amusing and harmless. So what's the problem? Nothing as long as you conduct yourself with the belief that superstitious objects and rituals – from broken mirrors to your daily horoscope – can't bring about good or bad luck. You aren't willing to let such notions and nonsense rule your life.

The danger of superstition lies in its ability to lure you into trusting it, thus allowing it some degree of influence over your life. In that case, it subverts God's rightful place.

Whether or not it's superstition, something does rule your life. It should be God – and God alone.

We broke that jinx over there.
-- Wingback Noble Doss on the 1941 win over Texas A&M

**Superstitions may not rule your life, but
something does; it should be God and God alone.**

DAY 53

PLAN AHEAD

Read Psalm 33:1-15.

"The plans of the Lord stand firm forever, the purposes of his heart through all generations" (v. 11).

The plan was to generate excitement for women's college basketball by matching the two best collegiate programs for a thrilling, down-to-the wire contest before the largest crowd in the history of the sport. Then the Texas women had to go and lay waste to all the careful planning.

The Tennessee athletic department cooked up a superpower summit between the Horns and the Vols on Dec. 9, 1987, in Knoxville. A ticket giveaway for this meeting of the sport's last two national champions was part of the plan to set a record for the size of the crowd. It worked so well that Tennessee head coach Pat Summitt got caught in a five-mile-long traffic jam and had to bail out of her car and hoof it to the arena.

There she found the place jammed with 24,563 fans. A representative from the Guinness World Records Museum confirmed that all the planning had achieved its goal: The crowd shattered the old record of 15,615. As it turned out, however, "the people were there, but the game didn't quite make it."

That's because the Longhorn women blew up all the planning for a close game by blasting the Volunteers 98-78 "in a display so cold, clinical and convincing that those groaning stands began emptying with seven minutes to go." Texas junior Clarissa Davis, the National Player of the Year in 1987 and 1989, dominated the game, pouring in a career high 45 points "with a brilliant blend of turnaround jumpers and power moves."

Texas head coach Jody Conradt was not at all contrite about up-setting the carefully laid plans. "It would have been better if the game had been closer," she admitted. "But there are limits that even I have for promoting the game."

Successful living takes planning. You go to school to improve your chances for a better paying job. You use blueprints to build your home. You save money and invest for retirement. You map out your vacation to cram the most fun into the least time. You even plan your children -- sometimes.

Your best-laid plans, however, sometime get wrecked by events and circumstances beyond your control. The economy goes into the tank; a debilitating illness strikes; a hurricane hits. Life is capricious and thus no plans -- not even your best ones -- are foolproof.

But you don't have to go it alone. God has plans for your life that guarantee success as God defines it if you will make him your planning partner. God's plan for your life includes joy, love, peace, kindness, gentleness, and faithfulness, all the elements necessary for truly successful living for today and for all eternity. And God's plan will not fail.

If you don't know where you are going, you will wind up somewhere else.

-- *Yogi Berra*

**Your plans may ensure a successful life;
God's plans will ensure a successful eternity.**

HEART OF THE MATTER

Read Matthew 6:19-24.

"Store up for yourselves treasures in heaven . . . . For where your treasure is, there your heart will be also" (vv. 20, 21).

They threw $4 million cash at him and $20 million overall, but the young man who once washed windows and scrubbed tile for spending money went with his heart and not his head.

In 1997, junior Ricky Williams led all of college football with 1,893 yards and 25 touchdowns and finished fifth in the Heisman Trophy balloting. As a team, however, the Longhorns did not fare as well, finishing 4-7. With each loss, speculation grew that head coach John Mackovic would be fired at the end of the season. Williams said he would leave Austin for the NFL if that happened. Waiting for him in the pros was a $20-million deal that included a $4 million signing bonus. The projected contract amounted to riches virtually beyond imagining for a young man who had worked on Sunday mornings before a local fast-food restaurant opened and earned $4.95 for his effort.

Everything began to change, however, in the season-ending loss to Texas A&M even though Mack Brown replaced Mackovic. Williams hurt his ankle during the game and felt that if he had been healthy, the Horns would have won. "I didn't want to end my career on a game like that," he said. An additional factor affecting his decision was how much he loved the University of Texas.

Still, the new head coach knew that the first recruit he had to snare was his star running back. They had a long conversation during which Williams finally asked Brown, "Coach, do I do what people tell me I should do, or do I do what in my heart I want to do?" Brown responded, "If you need the money right now, then you should go. If you don't, then do whatever it is that you really want to do."

Williams went with his heart and returned to Austin for his senior season. He broke the NCAA career rushing record, led the Horns to a 9-3 turnaround season, and won the Heisman Trophy.

As Ricky Williams did, we often face decisions that force us to choose between our heart and our head. Our head says take that job with the salary increase; our heart says don't relocate because the kids are doing so well. Our head declares now is not the time to start a relationship; our heart insists that we're in love.

We wrestle with our head and our heart as we determine what matters the most to us. When it comes to the ultimate priority in our lives, though, our head *and* our heart tell us it's Jesus.

What that means for our lives is a resolution of the conflict we face daily: That of choosing between the values of our culture and a life of trust in and obedience to God. The two may occasionally be compatible, but when they're not, our head tells us what Jesus wants us to do; our heart tells us how right it is that we do it.

If it's something that you really want to do in your heart, stick with it and work hard and just keep your faith in Christ.
-- All-Pro defensive back Ty Law

**In our struggle with competing value systems,
our head and our heart lead us to follow Jesus.**

PAIN RELIEF

Read 2 Corinthians 1:3-7.

"Just as the sufferings of Christ flow over into our lives, so also through Christ our comfort overflows" (v. 5).

His team obviously wasn't going to win without him, so Jerry Sisemore ignored the pain and went back into the game.

An offensive tackle, Sisemore was inducted into the College Football Hall of Fame in 2002. He started for the Horns as a sophomore in 1970 and was All-America both as a junior and a senior.

In a game against SMU, the press box spotter rather casually mentioned after another successful Longhorn running play that Sisemore had knocked down five guys on the play. Asked about it after the game, head coach Darrell Royal said, "He's really good, but I doubt if he did that." When Royal later saw the film, he realized the spotter was vindicated except that Sisemore indeed hadn't knocked down five guys on the play; it had been six.

Never was it more effectively demonstrated that Sisemore was the heart and soul of the offense than in the Baylor game of 1972. Through the first three quarters of the game, the Bears held the mighty Longhorn wishbone to 128 yards and a 3-3 tie. The problem with the offense was on the sideline because that's where Jerry Sisemore was. He had sprained an ankle in the first half and was out of the game -- or so it seemed.

As the fourth quarter started, Sisemore went to trainer Frank Medina, pointed to the ankle, and ordered, "Tape it." It took sev-

LONGHORNS

eral sessions, but he eventually limped to the coaches and told them, "I think I can go." The Longhorns had the ball at their own 30, and "there was Sisemore, half limping, half stalking his way onto the field." The Horns drove 70 yards in ten plays to lead 10-3. When they got the ball back, the hurting tackle pulled himself off the bench and went in again. This time they went 85 yards in 17 plays, Roosevelt Leaks following Sisemore into the end zone.

The Horns won 17-3, largely because Jerry Sisemore had the heart and the will to play with pain.

Since you live on Earth and not in Heaven, you are forced to play with pain. Whether it's a car wreck that left you shattered, the end of a relationship that left you battered, or a loved one's death that left you tattered -- pain finds you and challenges you to keep going.

While God's word teaches that you will reap what you sow, life also teaches that pain and hardship are not necessarily the result of personal failure. Pain in fact can be one of the tools God uses to mold your character and change your life.

What are you to do when you are hit full-speed by the awful pain that seems to choke the very will to live out of you? Where is your consolation, your comfort, and your help?

In almighty God, whose love will never fail. When life knocks you to your knees, you're closer to God than ever before.

In his white uniform and the heavy tape, Jerry Sisemore looked something like the abominable snowman cast against the gray November sky.
-- Writer Bill Little on the '72 Baylor game

When life hits you with pain, you can always turn to God for comfort, consolation, and hope.

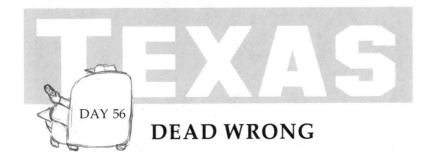

DAY 56

DEAD WRONG

Read Matthew 26:14-16; 27:1-10.

"When Judas, who had betrayed him, saw that Jesus was condemned, he was seized with remorse" (v. 27:3).

Probably no umpiring crew in history has been as wrong as the bunch that cost the Longhorns a shot at the national title by calling a runner out at first base when the ball was in right field.

In the 1969 College World Series, the Horns took on New York University for the right to advance to the national championship game. Texas trailed 3-2 with two outs in the top of the ninth, but catcher Tommy Harmon kept the team alive with a double. Center fielder Jack Miller then chopped a ball deep behind first base.

The NYU first baseman knocked the ball down, got it in his glove, and dived for the base as Harmon rounded third and Miller dived head first for the bag. The first baseman hit the bag a split second before Miller did, and the umpire called Miller out. The umps then hurried toward the dugouts as Harmon crossed home plate and Miller lay disconsolate in the dirt.

In the Texas bullpen, though, pitcher James Street was warming up when he noticed a ball rolling free down the right field line. "I couldn't figure out where it came from," he said. When the NYU right fielder hustled over and fielded the ball, it was fairly obvious where it had come from. The first baseman had dropped the ball.

Texas coach Cliff Gustafson raced out to the first-base umpire, shouting, "He dropped the ball." The umpire responded that he didn't. "Then what's the right fielder doing with it?" Gustafson asked. Puzzled, the umpire said, "Hey, fellas" and called his peers to a council. "A crowd of almost 10,000, the games committee, both teams, and even some animals in the Omaha zoo near the fence saw the ball roll away." But not one of the umps saw it, and because the play didn't involve a rule interpretation, the call stood.

There's wrong, there's dead wrong, and there's Judas wrong. We've all been wrong in our lives, but we can at least honestly ease our conscience by telling ourselves we'll never be as wrong as Judas was. A close examination of Judas' actions, however, reveals that we can indeed replicate in our own lives the mistake Judas made that drove him to suicidal despair.

Judas ultimately regretted his betrayal of our Lord, but his sorrow and remorse, however boundless, could not save him. His attempt to undo his initial wrong was futile because he tried to fix everything himself rather than turning to God in repentance and begging for mercy.

While we can't literally betray Jesus to his enemies as Judas did, we can match Judas' failure in our own lives by not turning to God in Jesus' name and asking for forgiveness for our sins. In that case, we ultimately will be as dead wrong as Judas was.

Texas was right -- dead right -- but on the most controversial play in the history of the College World Series, Texas was just as dead as if it had been dead wrong.
-- Writers Wilbur Evans and Bill Little on the '69 NYU game

A sin is the first wrong; failing to ask God
for forgiveness of it is the second.

MAKING UP

Read Matthew 5:21-24.

"If you are offering your gift at the altar and there remember that your brother has something against you, leave your gift there in front of the altar. First go and be reconciled to your brother" (vv. 23-24).

The formation of the Southwest Conference brought order to what had become a mess. It also led to a reconciliation between Texas and Texas A&M and the renewal of their football rivalry.

The driving force behind a new conference was UT's first-ever athletic director, Theo Bellmont, who arrived in 1913. He wrote to other large schools in the Southwest to determine their interest in forming a new athletic league. Officials from eight schools met in Dallas in May 1914 and laid the groundwork for what would become the Southwest Conference. A major obstacle, though, was Texas' objections to A&M head football coach Charley Moran.

Relationships between Texas and Texas A&M had been rocky for some time. In 1908, fans and students got into a brawl at half-time; one Texas fan received three stab wounds to his head in the scuffle. Relations went steadily downhill from there. Before the 1911 game, officials from both schools delivered assurances that the violence on the field and on the sidelines would be toned down.

It wasn't. Texas won 6-0, and afterwards, UT athletic chairman W.T. Mather notified A&M the 1912 game was off. Steve Pinckney, the Texas football team manager, accused Moran of teaching his players "that the only way to win a game is to slug and maim the star players of the opposing team." Athletic relations between the two schools were completely severed.

Only when A&M announced that Moran would not be back for the 1915 season was the new league formed. A&M and Texas met in 1915 and played each other annually until 2012.

College sports just wouldn't be as much fun if we didn't have rivalries with teams we love to insult, rail against, and whip the daylights out of. Our personal relationships are totally different, however, though sometimes a spirited disagreement with someone we love is worth it because the kissing and making up is so much fun.

Making up carries an inherent problem, however, because for that reconciliation to occur, somebody must make the first move, which is always the hardest one. So often relationships in our lives are fractured simply because no one has the courage to be the first to attempt to make things right. We hide behind our wounded pride or injured feelings and allow a priceless relationship to wither and die.

The model in such a situation is Jesus. He not only told us to offer a hand and a hug, he lived it, surrendering his life so we could all get right with God.

A&M has stretched forth the olive branch, and I believe we will be recreant if we do not seize up this opportunity to renew amicable relations.
— Engineering dean T.U. Taylor on renewing the rivalry with A&M

Reconciliation takes courage; just ask Jesus,
who died to get you right with God.

THE SUB

Read Galatians 3:10-14.

"Christ redeemed us from the curse of the law by becoming a curse for us" (v. 13).

The Horns appeared to have a legitimate shot at whipping the second-ranked Sooners in 1977 until both the starting quarterback and his backup went down before the first quarter was over. That left the game in the hands of an untested sub, which, as it turned out, was a good place to be.

Fred Akers' first Texas team roared out of the gates; the Horns ripped Boston College 44-0, buried Virginia 68-0, and slaughtered Rice 72-0 to soar up to a No. 5 national ranking. Next up, though, was Oklahoma; the Sooners had beaten Texas six straight times.

Oklahoma led 3-0 early on when Texas' chances for the upset took a severe hit -- or at least quarterback Mark McBath did. He suffered a season-ending broken ankle. Not to worry. Jon Aune, strong-armed and experienced, came in. Against Boston College, he had thrown a school-record 88-yard touchdown pass to senior wide receiver Alfred Jackson. But Aune promptly tripped over a Sooner lineman and tore knee ligaments.

Time now to worry. That left the game in the hands of third-string quarterback Randy McEachern, who the season before had watched the OU game from the press box as a spotter for the radio broadcasters. This "untested reserve with little playing experience" was about to join teammate Earl Campbell as a Longhorn legend.

He played the final 48 minutes of the pressure-packed game, leading a beautiful 80-yard drive in six plays for a 10-3 Texas lead that held up. Texas won 13-6, and McEachern's teammates carried him off the field. He started the rest of the season, quarterbacking the Horns to an 11-0 record and the No. 1 ranking. This sub who became a Longhorn folk hero in one afternoon was the starter in 1978 as a senior and still holds four school passing records.

Wouldn't it be cool if you had a sub like Randy McEachern for all of life's hard stuff? Telling of a death in the family? Call in your sub. Breaking up with your boyfriend? Job interview? Chemistry test? Crucial presentation at work? Let the sub handle it.

We do have such a substitute, but not for the matters of life. Instead, Jesus is our substitute for matters of life and death. Since Jesus has already made it, we don't have to make the sacrifice God demands for forgiveness and salvation.

One of the ironies of our age is that many people desperately grope for a substitute for Jesus. Mysticism, human philosophies such as Scientology, false religions such as Hinduism and Islam, cults, New Age approaches that preach self-fulfillment without responsibility or accountability – they and others like them are all pitiful, inadequate substitutes for Jesus.

Accept no substitutes. It's Jesus or nothing.

Randy [McEachern] came in and took it by the horns. He showed everybody how good he was.
                                        -- Defensive tackle Brad Shearer

**There is no substitute for Jesus,
the consummate substitute.**

DAY 59

BROKEN DREAMS

Read Joel 2:28-32.

"I will pour out my Spirit on all people. . . . Your old men will dream dreams" (v. 28).

The greatest dream of Jack Chevigny's life was snatched away from him just when it seemed to be coming true. One of Texas' most memorable upset wins was a result.

Chevigny scored the first touchdown for Notre Dame in the 12-6 upset of Army in 1928, the game that featured coach Knute Rockne's legendary "Win One for the Gipper" halftime speech. Rockne hand-picked Chevigny to be an assistant coach and later told him, "Chev, you're doing a fine job. . . . And when I leave here one day, you're going to be the head coach."

Rockne was killed in a plane crash in 1931. In a manner he never wanted, Chevigny was on the verge of seeing his dream come true. Notre Dame athletic officials, however, decided he was too young for the job and passed him over. Chevigny's dream was crushed; "he was bitterly heartbroken."

He left Notre Dame and was the head coach at St. Edwards University in Austin when Texas snatched him up to take over the Longhorn program in 1934. As the schedule would have it, the second game of Chevigny's first season was against Notre Dame, which had won two straight national titles and was riding a 26-game win streak.

In his pregame speech, Chevigny invoked Rockne, his dead

mother, and even his "doddering father, who was valiantly holding death at bay long enough to know whether his boy would whip the [school that] had done him wrong. . . . By kickoff, the Texas players were frothing."

The Irish fumbled the opening kickoff, and Jack Gray, who would be an All-American basketball player, recovered on the 18. Four plays later, Bohn Hilliard followed right guard Joe Smartt on an 8-yard touchdown run. The gritty Longhorns made the lone score stand up for the 7-6 win that "signaled the arrival of the Southwest Conference as a major player on the national scene."

Like Jack Chevigny, we all have particular dreams. Perhaps to make a million dollars, write the Great American Novel, or find the perfect spouse. More likely than not, though, we gradually lose our hold on those dreams. They slip away from us as we surrender them to the reality of everyday living.

But we also have general dreams. For world peace. For an end to hunger. That no child is ever afraid again. These dreams we hold doggedly onto as if something inside us tells us that even though the world gets itself into a bigger mess every year, one day everything will be all right.

That's because it will be. God has promised a time when his spirit will rule the world. Jesus spoke of a time when he will return to claim his kingdom. In that day, our dreams of peace and plenty and the banishment of hate and want will be reality.

Our dreams based on God's promises will come true.

We did it. We won. [We] beat Notre Dame. A dream come true.
-- Jack Chevigny as fans and players hoisted him onto their shoulders

Dreams based on God's promises will come true.

WHAT A SURPRISE!

Read 1 Thessalonians 5:1-11.

"You, brothers, are not in darkness so that this day should surprise you like a thief" (v. 4).

Larry Robinson didn't even consider playing for a "basketball" school because he just didn't believe he was good enough for a basketball career. Boy, was he in for a surprise.

"What I really wanted was a good education," Robinson said about choosing a college. "I couldn't see myself playing pro ball. I didn't see how I could make it." Leon Black, who had played guard for the Longhorns in the 1950s, had been hired in 1967 to return the program to the glory days it had enjoyed under Jack Gray in the 1940s. Still, Black was hampered by a limited budget and antiquated Gregory Gym, which seated only 7,800. Thus, Texas was anything but a basketball powerhouse.

So, seeing himself "as an ordinary man seeking an education" and not as a young man with a future in basketball, Robinson opted for Austin. He arrived on campus in 1970 and produced a freshman season that was a complete surprise, especially to him. He rewrote the freshman record books by averaging 33.9 points per game.

As a sophomore, Robinson was named the Southwest Conference's Player of the Year. After he lost most of his junior season to a knee injury, Robinson returned with a vengeance as a senior. He averaged 22.5 points and 10.9 rebounds per game and again was the league's Player of the Year. When Robinson left Texas in 1974, he had broken all but one of Texas' major scoring and rebounding records.

About that pro career. Robinson signed with a Swedish team for the highest sum ever paid to a basketball player and had a great career that included multiple championships and MVP awards. Much to his surprise.

Surprise birthday parties are a delight. And what's the fun of opening Christmas presents when we already know what's in them? Some surprises in life provide us with experiences that are both joyful and delightful.

Generally, though, we expend energy and resources to avoid most surprises and the impact they may have upon our lives. We may be surprised by the exact timing of a baby's arrival, but we nevertheless have the bags packed beforehand and the nursery all set for its occupant. Paul used this very image (v. 3) to describe the Day of the Lord, when Jesus will return to claim his own and establish his kingdom. We may be caught by surprise, but we must still be ready.

The consequences of being caught unprepared by a baby's insistence on being born are serious indeed. They pale, however, beside the eternal effects of not being ready when Jesus returns. We prepare ourselves just as Paul told us to (v. 8): We live in faith, hope, and love, ever on the alert for that great, promised day.

Surprise me.
-- Yogi Berra on where his wife should have him buried

**The timing of Jesus' return will be a surprise;
the consequences should not be.**

I CAN'T STAND IT!

Read Exodus 32:1-20.

"[Moses'] anger burned and he threw the tablets out of his hands, breaking them to pieces at the foot of the mountain" (v. 19).

How in the world can a football season in which the Horns won twelve games and the Fiesta Bowl and finished with a No.-3 national ranking be frustrating? Because of circumstances beyond the team's control, they didn't get the shot they deserved at a league or a national championship.

Texas began the 2008 season ranked No. 10 in the nation and steadily moved up week after week. The highlight of the season was a 45-35 win over top-ranked Oklahoma that propelled the Horns into the No.-1 spot for the first time in the regular season since 1984. Wins over ranked Missouri and Oklahoma State followed. Then a one-point loss to Texas Tech in the last second of the game cost the Horns that lofty ranking. As the season played out, the loss also cost the Horns much more.

Viewed as a whole, the season was a magnificent one as the Horns beat five teams ranked in the Top 20. Quarterback Colt McCoy set an all-time record for pass completion percentage. The Horns passed Notre Dame as the second-winningest program in NCAA history.

And yet -- what may well have been the best football team in the country didn't get a chance to prove it on the field. When the Big 12 South ended in a three-way tie, the tiebreaker went to the team that finished highest in the BCS standings. That was Oklahoma, even though Texas had soundly whipped the Sooners. The Horns were thus frustratingly shut out of both the Big 12 championship game and the BCS title game.

So they went to the Fiesta Bowl and whipped Ohio State 24-21 on a pass with 16 seconds left from McCoy to Quan Cosby.

The traffic light catches you when you're running late for work or your doctor's appointment. The bureaucrat gives you red tape when you want assistance. Your daughter refuses to take her homework seriously. Makes your blood boil, doesn't it?

Frustration is part of God's testing ground that is life, even if much of what frustrates us today results from man-made organizations, bureaucracies, and machines. What's important is not that you encounter frustration—that's a given—but how you handle it. Do you respond with curses, screams, and violence? Or with a deep breath, a silent prayer, and calm persistence, and patience?

It may be difficult to imagine Jesus stuck in traffic or waiting for hours in a long line in a government office. It is not difficult, however, to imagine how he would act in such situations, and, thus, to know exactly how you should respond. No matter how frustrated you are.

A life of frustration is inevitable for any coach whose main enjoyment is winning.
-- NFL Hall of Fame coach Chuck Noll

Frustration is a vexing part of life,
but God expects us to handle it gracefully.

COMEBACK KIDS

Read Psalm 51.

"Create in me a pure heart, O God, and renew a steadfast spirit within me. . . . Restore to me the joy of your salvation and grant me a willing spirit" (vv. 10, 12).

The Longhorn baseball team once pulled a comeback so legendary that the contest in which it occurred has simply become known as The Game.

On May 10, 1962, Texas hosted Texas A&M in a game that would decide the conference championship, the winner playing on, the loser's season over. A&M jumped out to an early 9-2 lead and was ahead 9-3 as Texas batted in the bottom of the eighth.

After a leadoff walk, Buddy New, whom coach Bibb Falk had put in "to give him a chance to letter," blasted one onto Billy Goat Hill. (See Devotion No. 40.) While the Aggies scrambled to get to the ball, New lumbered all the way around for an inside-the-park home run. Before the inning ended, the Horns added three more runs on infield ground balls and a bases-loaded walk. The Longhorns trailed only 9-8 headed into the ninth.

The Aggies scored a run in the top of the ninth to lead 10-8, and hopes for a Longhorn comeback dimmed when the first two batters were retired in the bottom of the frame. But then Bill Bethea walked, and Pat Rigby, the team's leading hitter, drilled a double and advanced to third when the throw got away from the catcher. Ed Kasper hit a chopper to deep short and the shortstop

LONGHORNS

couldn't make a play. Rigby scored and the game was tied.

With two outs in the bottom of the tenth, New did it again, slamming a double. Gary London then drilled one to the cliff in deep left center. "When the ball was hit, the crowd of 4,000, the ghosts of every Texas baseball player who ever was or ever will be, rose as one." New scored easily for the 11-10 win and was mobbed at the plate. While Texas A&M went home, the comeback kids went on to finish third in the College World Series.

Life will have its setbacks whether they result from personal failures or from forces and people beyond your control. Being a Christian and a faithful follower of Jesus Christ doesn't insulate you from getting into deep trouble.

Maybe financial problems suffocated you. A serious illness put you on the sidelines. Or your family was hit with a great tragedy. Life is a series of victories and defeats. Winning isn't about avoiding defeat; it's about getting back up to compete again. It's about making a comeback of your own.

When you cast your fate upon God's mercy, forgiveness, and cleansing power as King David did, your comeback is always greater than your setback. You are never too far behind, and it's never too late in life's game for Jesus to lead you to victory, to turn trouble into triumph.

As it was with the Longhorns of 1962 against A&M and with David, it's not how you start that counts; it's how you finish.

Now how's that for a comeback?
-- UT official scorer Orland Sims on the '62 A&M game

In life, victory is truly a matter of how you finish
and whether you finish with Jesus at your side.

REVELATION

Read Isaiah 53.

"But he was pierced for our transgressions, he was crushed for our iniquities; the punishment that brought us peace was upon him, and by his wounds we are healed" (v. 5).

Riding on the team bus to what many considered the biggest game in the history of college football, Darrell Royal revealed himself to be not just a coach but a little bit of a prophet also.

When Texas and Arkansas met on Dec. 6, 1969, the Horns were No. 1 and the Hogs were No. 2. The game was so big that President Richard Nixon announced he would attend and present a plaque to the winner that recognized the team as the national champion. Billy Graham gave the pregame invocation.

On the bus ride to the stadium, Royal called James Street, his quarterback, up to the front. He then surprised Street by telling him what he wanted to do if the Horns fell behind by fourteen points late in the game. "When we score the first time, I want to go for two and here's the play I want you to run," Royal said. The senior QB felt there was no way the Horns could fall two touchdowns behind, but he noted what his coach said.

Incredibly, just as Royal had foreseen, Arkansas led 14-0 when the third quarter ended. On the first play of the final period, Street scrambled his way to a 42-yard touchdown. Again, just as Royal had envisioned, the Longhorns went for two. Street called the predetermined play, option left, and scored. Later came what has been called "perhaps the most significant play in Texas history." On fourth and three from the Texas 43, Street threw a perfect pass to tight end Randy Peschel to the Hog 13. Two plays later, sophomore halfback Jim Bertelsen scored from the two. Happy Feller booted the PAT.

Texas won 15-14 to win the national championship, thanks in large part to the two-point conversion Royal had envisioned.

In our jaded age, we have relegated prophecy to dark rooms in which mysterious women peer into crystal balls or clasp our sweaty palms while uttering some vague generalities. At best, we understand a prophet as someone who predicts future events.

Within the pages of the Bible, though, we encounter something radically different. A prophet is a messenger from God, one who relays divine revelation to others.

Prophets seem somewhat foreign to us because in one very real sense the age of prophecy is over. In the name of Jesus, we have access to God through our prayers and through scripture. In searching for God's will for our lives, we seek divine revelation. We may speak only for ourselves and not for the greater body of Christ, but we do not need a prophet to discern what God would have us do. We need faith in the one whose birth, life, and death fulfilled more than 300 Bible prophecies.

I gave up a long time ago trying to predict the future and trying to deal with things I couldn't deal with.

-- Brett Favre

**Persons of faith continuously seek a word
from God for their lives.**

AT A LOSS

Read Philippians 3:1-9.

"I consider everything a loss compared to the surpassing greatness of knowing Christ Jesus my Lord, for whose sake I have lost all things" (v. 8).

When the Longhorn football team loses, the UT faithful take it to heart, often plunging deep into the pit of despair. It's nothing new; some of the players on the 1894 team took a loss to Missouri so hard they quit school and never played football again.

Texas fielded its first team in 1893. (See Devotion No. 1.) These hardy, feisty pioneers let their hair grow long and bushy to protect their heads in the absence of helmets. The first-ever game was an 18-16 win over the Dallas Football Club. When the game ended, John Henry "Baby" Myers, the team's biggest man at 210 pounds, wasn't ready to stop playing. "Why are we quitting now?" he asked teammate and tackle James Morrison, who scored Texas' first-ever touchdown. "It's nowhere near sundown."

The game was quite different back then. The *Dallas News* wrote, "The professional game of foot ball [*sic*] looks very much like an Indian wrestling match with a lot of running thrown in." However this new game was being played, those lads from Austin were pretty good at it. Appropriately -- hey, this *is* UT -- the first squad went undefeated at 4-0. The second team ripped off six straight wins, including the first-ever defeats of Texas A&M, Tulane, and Arkansas.

LONGHORNS

The season ended with a game against Missouri. "We were getting pretty swell-headed by the time Missouri came along," said the first Longhorn star, Ad Day. After all, Texas had never lost a game. Missouri took care of that. According to Day, they "came along and tore up our line like it wasn't there."

After the 28-0 loss, some of the Texas players cut their hair short so folks wouldn't know they had been on the team. Some, including Day, quit both school and football permanently.

Maybe, it was when a family member died. Perhaps it wasn't so staggeringly tragic: your puppy died, your best friend moved away, or an older sibling left home. Like those pioneer Texas football players, sometime in your youth or early adult life, you learned that loss is a part of life.

Loss inevitably diminishes your life, but loss and the grief that accompanies it are part of the price of loving. When you first encountered loss, you learned that you were virtually helpless to prevent it or escape it.

There is life after loss, though, because you have one sure place to turn. Jesus can share your pain and ease your suffering; but he doesn't stop there. Through the loss of his own life, he has transformed death -- the ultimate loss -- into the ultimate gain of eternal life. In Jesus lies the promise that one day loss itself will die.

I sneaked out of town that night and cut out my 'football course' at The University of Texas.
-- Ad Day on his reaction to the Missouri loss

**Jesus not only eases the pain of our losses
but transforms the loss caused by death
into the gain of eternal life.**

FEAR FACTOR

Read Matthew 14:22-33.

"[The disciples] cried out in fear. But Jesus immediately said to them: 'Take courage! It is I. Don't be afraid'" (vv. 26-27).

Kathleen Nash was so fearless that even after she broke her nose in practice, she refused to wear a mask in games.

Nash finished her career in Austin with the 2010-11 season. A 6-2 guard, she specialized in the rather unusual combination of rebounding and three-point shots. She was the first player in the history of Texas women's basketball to score 1,000 points, snare 700 rebounds, and hit 200 three-point field goals. She is second all-time in the Longhorn record book for career three-pointers and career free-throw percentage.

At one point during her senior season, Nash "looked like she had gone a couple [of] rounds with Rocky Balboa." While she was preparing for the Kansas game of Feb. 5, she broke her nose during a scrimmage when it lost the battle with a teammate's swinging elbow. This was only a week after she suffered a black eye in practice. The fearless Nash refused to wear a mask to protect her nose. Only when she broke it again against Iowa State did she relent.

The black eye healed quickly, but the nose remained bruised and swollen through the end of the season, a testament to her fearless and relentless drive to grab rebounds. "It's been a tough season," Nash admitted, "tougher than all the ones before this."

Nash was fearless even as a child. When she was only 4, she challenged her older sister, Kristen, a forward for Texas who also completed her college play in 2010-11, to an arm wrestling match. "Kat would beat me like it was no big deal," Kristen recalled. "And then she'd beat my brother Michael, who was 7 at the time."

Kathleen Nash took that early trait of fearlessness right on to a collegiate career that had her described as "one of the most distinguished basketball players in University of Texas history."

Some fears are universal; others are particular. Speaking to the Rotary Club may require a heavy dose of antiperspirant. Elevator walls may feel as though they're closing in on you. And don't even get started on being in the dark with spiders and snakes during a thunderstorm.

We all live in fear, and God knows this. Dozens of passages in the Bible urge us not to be afraid. God isn't telling us to lose our wariness of oncoming cars or big dogs with nasty dispositions; this is a helpful fear God instilled in us for protection.

What God does wish driven from our lives is a spirit of fear that dominates us, that makes our lives miserable and keeps us from doing what we should, such as sharing our faith. In commanding that we not be afraid, God reminds us that when we trust completely in him, we find peace that calms our fears.

Let me win. But if I cannot win, let me be brave in the attempt.
— Special Olympics Motto

You have your own peculiar set of fears,
but they should never paralyze you
because God is greater than anything you fear.

HOW YOU SEE IT

Read John 20:11-18.

"Mary stood outside the tomb crying" (v. 11).

We've got them right where we want them," declared Texas All-American linebacker Johnny Treadwell. At the moment, Arkansas fans could very well have said the same thing with equal conviction. It all depended on your perspective.

Both Texas and Arkansas were 4-0 when they met at Memorial Stadium on Oct. 20, 1962. The heart of the top-ranked Horns team was its defense, led by defensive tackle Scott Appleton, linebacker Pat Culpepper, end Knox Nunnally, and Treadwell. The defense dominated, but sixth-ranked Arkansas led 3-0 at halftime; Texas had only one first down in the first half.

Arkansas put together a last-half drive that exasperated Treadwell no end because the Razorbacks just kept chunking the ball. "He was tired of them throwing for first downs," said Culpepper. "He thought they'd run out of room and would have to come right at us." But Arkansas kept throwing and kept moving, all the way to the Longhorn 5.

That's when Treadwell delivered his unique perspective on the situation, announcing that the Longhorn defense had the Razorbacks right where it wanted them. Knowing that a touchdown would pretty much wrap the game up, Arkansas' players and fans must have felt the same way.

On third down, Arkansas' 218-lb. fullback headed into the line, just as Treadwell wanted. He and Culpepper were ready, meeting the big bruiser head-on. The ball squirted loose, and Texas' Joe Dixon recovered.

The goal-line stand was captured in one of the most famous of all Longhorn photographs. With only 36 seconds left in the game, Tommy Ford bulled into the end zone for a 7-3 win that propelled the Longhorns to the conference championship.

Treadwell's perspective had been right; the Horns had had the Razorbacks right where they wanted them.

Your perspective goes a long way toward determining whether you slink through life amid despair, anger, and hopelessness or stride boldly through life with joy and hope. Mary Magdalene is an excellent example. On that first Easter morning, she stood by Jesus' tomb crying, her heart broken, because she still viewed everything through the perspective of Jesus' death. But how her attitude, her heart, and her life changed when she saw the morning through the perspective of Jesus' resurrection.

So it is with life and death for all of us. You can't avoid death, but you can determine how you perceive it. Is it fearful, dark, fraught with peril and uncertainty? Or is it a simple little passageway to glory, the light, and loved ones, an elevator ride to paradise?

It's a matter of perspective that depends totally on whether or not you're standing by Jesus' side when it arrives.

[Johnny Treadwell and Pat Culpepper] just loved goal-line defenses. They wanted you down there where you had to run right at them.
— Texas center/defensive tackle David McWilliams

Whether death is your worst enemy or a solicitous chauffeur is a matter of perspective.

PARTY ANIMALS

Read Exodus 14:26-31; 15:19-21.

"Miriam the prophetess, Aaron's sister, took a tambourine in her hand, and all the women followed her, with tambourines and dancing" (v. 15:20).

Imperturbable as always, Bevo was about the only one who didn't go bonkers as the Longhorns threw a party.

The cheerleaders, the band, Bevo, a whole bunch of fans, and the football team were in Darrell K. Royal-Texas Memorial Stadium. The scoreboard was even lit up. But the score never changed on this day, and the players wore jeans not pads because the occasion wasn't a football game. Instead, it was a party on Jan. 15, 2006, to celebrate the national championship and to honor the national champions after the defeat of USC in the Rose Bowl.

More than 50,000 adoring fans showed up for the party to bathe in the joy, cheer with and listen to their heroes, and gaze endlessly at the scoreboard that was permanently set to read Texas 41 USC 38. The party actually began at 6:30 p.m., but the party-goers started lining up outside the stadium about 7 a.m. Anticipating the wait, one family showed up with a 40-foot sub while others used cell phones to order pizzas, giving a gate number as the delivery site.

"It was madness," said a fan who came with three of his nephews. But then he added, "It was euphoria." In the crowd were some former teammates of the champs. "I'm mad I'm not still on the team," declared a grinning Tien Nguyen, who finished his play at defensive back in 2003.

The crowd knew how to party; they were raucous from the get-go and never lightened up. They jumped to their feet and cheered as the stadium's jumbo television showed highlights of the season. The loudest cheer was reserved, though, for the team itself, which showed up amid swirling smoke.

All in all, it was a party worthy of the national champions.

You know what it takes to throw a good party. You start with your closest friends, add some salsa and chips, fire up the grill and throw on some burgers and dogs, and then top it all off with the Longhorns' game on TV. You probably also know that just about any old excuse will do just fine to get people together for a party. All you really need is a sense that life is pretty good right now.

That's the thing about having Jesus as part of your life: He turns every day into a celebration of the good life. No matter what tragedies or setbacks life may have in store -- and they will come -- the heart given to Jesus will find the joy in living.

That's because such a life is spent with quiet confidence in God's promise of salvation through Jesus, a confidence that inevitably bubbles up into a joy the troubles of the world cannot touch. When a life is celebrated with Jesus, the party never stops.

This is one night when we can Hook 'em and take down the little finger, because we're number one.
— Mack Brown at the national championship party

With Jesus, life is one big party because it becomes a celebration of victory and joy.

ONE TOUGH COOKIE

Read 2 Corinthians 11:21b-29.

"Besides everything else, I face daily the pressure of my concern for all the churches" (v. 28).

Hubert "Hub" Bechtol was so tough that he once played in a football game with a broken jaw.

Bechtol started his college football career at Texas Tech in 1943 where he earned Little All-America honors and played on the basketball team. After he volunteered for the Navy and its V-12 program, he was ordered to the University of Texas in 1944 and became Texas' first three-time consensus All-America.

Bechtol played both ways at end. He was an excellent receiver and a devastating tackler. In the 34-7 blowout of SMU in 1944, he showed just how tough he was. He knocked SMU's best back out of the game with a piledriving tackle that also left him dazed. "I hit him right on his knee with my jaw," Bechtol recalled. The force of the blow knocked the bridge out of his mouth, and he lay on the ground for about five minutes while his teammates looked for it.

Bechtol took a break but went back in and played despite the pain. After the game, though, he realized something was amiss. "I picked up a potato chip, and I couldn't even crack it," he said.

His jaw was fractured in two places. He had it wired shut, but undid the device after a few minutes of discomfort. While he was in the hospital, his fiancee brought him a chocolate cake from his mother, and Bechtol said he "stuffed the cake between the crevices of my teeth."

In 1945, this legendary tough guy set a Longhorn single-season record with seven touchdown receptions. He caught nine passes in the Longhorns' 40-27 win over Missouri in the 1946 Cotton Bowl, for which he was honored with Bobby Layne as the game's Co-MVP.

You don't have to be a legendary Texas lineman to be tough. In America today, toughness isn't restricted to physical accomplishments and brute strength. Going to work every morning even when you feel bad, sticking by your rules for your children in a society that ridicules parental authority, making hard decisions about your aging parents' care often over their objections — you've got to be tough every day just to live honorably, decently, and justly.

Living faithfully requires toughness, too, though in America chances are you won't be imprisoned, stoned, or flogged this week for your faith as Paul was. Still, contemporary society exerts subtle, psychological, daily pressures on you to turn your back on your faith and your values. Popular culture promotes promiscuity, atheism, and gutter language; your children's schools have kicked God out; the corporate culture advocates amorality before the shrine of the almighty dollar.

You have to hang tough to keep the faith.

Darrell Royal told me once I hit him harder than anyone.
— Hubert Bechtol

**Life demands more than mere physical toughness;
you must be spiritually tough too.**

FAMILY TIES

Read Mark 3:31-35.

*"[Jesus] said, 'Here are my mother and my brothers!
Whoever does God's will is my brother and sister and
mother'" (vv. 34-35).*

The University of Texas women's tennis national champions
of 1993 and 1995 were certainly powerhouse teams who were all
about winning. In entirely different ways, though, each team was
also equally about family.

"This team is a family," Texas head coach Jeff Moore declared
after his Horns won the 1995 title. "There is talent, but in order
to be successful, you need to come together as a team." That '95
team/family posted a 26-3 record and won the program's eighth
straight Southwest Conference championship. Kelly Pace, who set
UT records for wins in a season (42) and career wins (152), was the
SWC Player of the Year. Pace, senior Lucie Ludvigova, sophomore
Farley Taylor, and freshman Cristina Moros were All-Americas.
Indiana, Arizona State, Stanford, and top-seeded Florida fell to
the second-seeded Longhorn family in the NCAA Tournament.

Family ties also served to inspire the 1993 national champs. On
the eve of the NCAA Tournament quarterfinals, Moore received
a phone call from his mother, who told him that his father's pan-
creatic cancer was worse. He had perhaps two weeks to live.

Moore did not hesitate. "It was an instant decision," he said. At
a team meeting, Moore told his players he would be leaving. "I felt

I needed to be home," he said. "[Dad's] time was so short." "We all felt for him," said senior Vickie Paynter, a four-time All-America. "We definitely wanted him to be with his family. [Before the match] we sat down and prayed for his father."

Knowing his Longhorns were ready, Moore turned the team over to first-year assistant Vicki Ellis, a former Texas star, and volunteer assistant Lea Sauls. He went home to be with his family while his tennis family won the NCAA title.

Some wit said families are like fudge, mostly sweet with a few nuts. You can probably call the names of your sweetest relatives, whom you cherish, and of the nutty ones too, whom you mostly try to avoid at a family reunion.

Like it or not, you have a family, and that's God's doing. God cherishes the family so much that he chose to live in one as a son, a brother, and a cousin.

One of Jesus' more startling actions was to redefine the family. No longer is it a single household of blood relatives or even a clan or a tribe. Jesus' family is the result not of an accident of birth but rather a conscious choice. All those who do God's will are members of Jesus' family.

What a startling and downright wonderful thought! You have family members out there you don't even know who stand ready to love you just because you're part of God's family.

I knew it was hard because [Coach Jeff Moore] wanted to be there so badly, but families are more important.
-- Jackie Moe, four-time tennis All-America

For followers of Jesus, family comes not from a shared ancestry but from a shared faith.

ANIMAL MAGNETISM

Read Psalm 139:1-18.

"For you created my inmost being; you knit me together in my mother's womb. I praise you because I am fearfully and wonderfully made" (vv. 13-14).

Before there was Bevo, there was Pig.

The first living longhorn steer mascot debuted at halftime of the 1916 Texas A&M game. When World War I broke out, he was forgotten and left on the farm. His end came ignominiously when he was the main course at a banquet honoring the 1920 team.

Before and during that time, however, the school had another "official" and much more beloved mascot, a tan and white pit bull mix named Pig. Theo Bellmont, UT's first athletic director, brought the dog to the campus when he was a 7-week-old puppy. He was named after the football team's center, Gus "Pig" Dittmar. During a 1914 game, they stood side by side on the sideline, and someone noticed they were both bowlegged.

An instant hit, Pig pretty much had the run of the campus. "Every morning, Pig greeted students and faculty on his daily rounds," related Jim Nicar, director of the UT Heritage Society. According to Nicar, Pig often visited classrooms and frequented the library on cold days. He regularly attended both home and away athletic events. Legend has it he snarled "at the slightest mention" of Texas A&M.

On New Year's Day 1923, Pig was struck by a car and died a

few days later. He lay in state in the front of the Co-Op in a casket draped with orange and white ribbon. Hundreds turned out to pay their respects. The Longhorn Band led the funeral procession to Pig's burial site near the old law building.

The University went without a mascot until 1932 when Bevo II was introduced, though the steer did not become a fixture at UT football games until 1966.

Animals such as Bevo and Pig elicit our awe and respect and often our love. Nothing enlivens a trip more than glimpsing turkeys, bears, or deer in the wild. Admit it: You go along with the kids' trip to the zoo because you think it's a cool place too. All that variety of life is mind-boggling. Who could conceive of a longhorn steer, a walrus, a moose, or a prairie dog? Who could possibly have that rich an imagination?

But the next time you're in a crowd, look around at the parade of faces. Who could come up with the idea for all those different people, let alone for the billions of people who inhabit this planet? For that matter, who could conceive of you? You are unique, a masterpiece who will never be duplicated.

The master creator, God Almighty, is behind it all. He thought of you and then brought you into being. If you had a manufacturer's label, it might say, "Lovingly, fearfully, and wonderfully handmade in Heaven by #1 -- God."

Pig's Dead -- Dog Gone

-- Inscription on Pig's tombstone

**You may consider some painting
or a magnificent animal a work of art,
but the real masterpiece is you.**

MIRACLE PLAY

Read Matthew 12:38-42.

"He answered, 'A wicked and adulterous generation asks for a miraculous sign!'" (v. 39)

Somehow, you had to believe they had one last miracle left in them." And so they did.

Until Jan. 1, 2005, the Rose Bowl had never been decided on the last play of the game. That all changed when the Texas Longhorns pulled off that miracle.

Six times that season the Horns had come from behind to win, including overcoming a 35-7 deficit to Oklahoma State. Even more miraculous was the 14 points they scored and the improbable first down on fourth and 18 they converted, all in the last five minutes, to beat Kansas 27-23.

In the Rose Bowl, the Horns were in trouble again. After Vince Young did his "Texas Two-Step" for 60 yards and a touchdown, Michigan scored 17 straight points to lead 31-21, the last three coming on a field goal with 2:35 to go in the third quarter. But the Wolverines couldn't contain Young. Before the night was over, he would rush for 192 yards and four touchdowns and would pass for 180 yards and another score. He led the Horns back from the brink, scoring on a 10-yard scramble with 9:51 to play. ABC announcer Keith Jackson asked, "How in the world?" as Young crossed the goal line. Then with 4:56 left, Young scored again.

But Texas still needed one last miracle play after the Wolverines answered with a field goal with 3:04 left. So here came Young and the Horns, covering 47 yards in ten plays. With two seconds left, they called on Dusty Mangum to provide the miracle finish with a 37-yard field goal. By the time his kick wobbled over the crossbar, the clock had ticked down to zero. Right about that time, the scoreboard changed to 38-37. Texas.

One last miracle in a night filled with them.

Miracles defy rational explanation -- like continually pulling off comebacks against a powerhouse football team. Or escaping with minor abrasions from an accident that totals your car. Or recovering from an illness that seemed terminal. Underlying the notion of miracles is the idea that they are rare instances of direct divine intervention that reveal God.

But life shows us quite the contrary, that miracles are anything but rare. Since God made the world and everything in it, everything around you is miraculous. Even you are a miracle.

Your life thus can be mundane, dull, and ordinary, or it can be spent in a glorious attitude of childlike wonder and awe. It depends on whether or not you see the world through the eyes of faith. Only through faith can you discern the hand of God in any event; only through faith can you see the miraculous and thus see God.

Jesus knew that miracles don't produce faith, but rather faith produces miracles.

Do you believe in miracles? Yes!
– Al Michaels when U.S. beat USSR in hockey in 1980 Winter Games.

Miracles are all around us, but it takes
the eyes of faith to see them.

STAR POWER

Read Luke 10:1-3, 17-20.

"The Lord appointed seventy-two others and sent them two by two ahead of him to every town and place where he was about to go" (v. 1).

The 1965 Orange Bowl was loaded with star power, and on the pivotal play of the game, Texas' star shone brighter than Alabama's did.

The Crimson Tide came into the game already crowned as the national champions of 1964 in a time when the polls determined the champ before the bowl games were played. Alabama was led by quarterback Joe Namath; on the Texas side, the undisputed star of the team was All-American linebacker Tommy Nobis. (See Devotion No. 99.)

Namath was as good as advertised, but the Longhorn offense didn't back down. Senior running back Ernie Koy, Jr. broke off a 79-yard touchdown run, and quarterback Jim Hudson hit wide receiver George Sauer with a 69-yard bomb. (Hudson and Sauer would go on to play for the New York Jets with Namath.) The Longhorns led 21-17 as the game wound down.

With a little more than six minutes left to play, the Tide faced fourth down at the Texas one-yard line. Bear Bryant eschewed the field goal and went for the touchdown, relying on his star. Namath tried a quarterback sneak. Tackle Tom Currie got penetration and disrupted the play, and linebacker Frank Bedrick hit Namath at the line. Namath didn't go down, though, sliding off to the side. There, Texas' own star, Nobis, rose up, slammed into Namath, and stopped him cold just short of the goal line.

The Longhorns won 21-17 and completed the season with a 10-1 record. The Orange-Bowl victory also finished a remarkable four-season run by the Longhorns of 40-2-1.

Football teams are like other organizations in that they may have a star but the star would be nothing without the supporting cast. It's the same in a private company, in a government bureaucracy, in a military unit, and just about any other team of people with a common goal.

That includes the team known as a church. It may have its "star" in the preacher, who is – like the quarterback or the company CEO – the most visible representative of the team. Preachers are, after all, God's paid, trained professionals.

But when Jesus assembled a team of seventy-two folks, he didn't have anybody on the payroll or any seminary graduates. All he had were no-names who loved him. And nothing has changed. God's church still depends on those whose only pay is the satisfaction of serving and whose only qualification is their love for God.

God's church needs you.

You may have the greatest bunch of individual stars in the world, but if they don't play together, the club won't be worth a dime.

— Babe Ruth

**Yes, the church needs its professional clergy,
but it also needs those who serve as volunteers
because they love God; the church needs you.**

TEN TO REMEMBER

Read Exodus 20:1-17.

"God spoke all these words: 'I am the Lord your God . . . .
You shall have no other gods before me'" (vv. 1, 3).

The win over Michigan State in 2003 that propelled the Horns to the Final four for the third time topped a 2006 list of the best moments in Longhorn men's basketball history. The top 10 from that list are especially worth remembering.

The selection of UT basketball's most golden moments was part of a promotion celebrating 100 years of Texas basketball. That 85-76 win over the Spartans that was chosen No. 1 meant the Horns were in the Final Four for the first time since 1947.

No. 2 was the 54-50 defeat of City College of New York in Madison Square Garden in 1947. This was the NCAA's third-place game and remains the highest national finish in school history.

Third on the list was the 44 consecutive wins from 1913-17. (See Devotion No. 94.) Number 4 was the 101-93 defeat of NC State on March 21, 1978, to win the championship of the NIT.

The fifth most celebrated moment occurred on April 12, 2003, when sophomore guard T.J. Ford won the John R. Wooden Player of the Year Award. Ford was the first player in UT history to be named the national player of the year.

No. 6 on the list was the 59-55 win over Washington in the NCAA regional finals on March 26, 1943. The win sent the Horns into the national semifinals. No. 7 is the induction of Slater Martin into the Basketball Hall of Fame in 1982. He is the only Longhorn to accomplish the feat.

Chosen the eighth most golden moment was the appearance in the Final Four in 2003, UT's first Final Four in modern history. No. 9 on the list was the 102-89 win over Xavier in the 1990 regional semi-finals. The tenth greatest moment was the 85-74 upset of Houston in 1972 in a first-round NCAA game, ending the Cougars' dominance of the Southwest Conference.

For Longhorn basketball fans, these are ten to remember .

You've got your list and you're ready to go: a gallon of paint and a water hose from the hardware store; chips, peanuts, and sodas from the grocery store for watching tonight's football game; the tickets for the band concert. Your list helps you remember.

God also made a list once of things he wanted you to remember; it's called the Ten Commandments. Just as your list reminds you to do something, so does God's list remind you of how you are to act in your dealings with other people and with him.

A life dedicated to Jesus is a life devoted to relationships, and God's list emphasizes that the social life and the spiritual life of the faithful cannot be sundered. God's relationship to you is one of unceasing, unqualified love, and you are to mirror that divine love in your relationships with others. In case you forget, you have a list.

Society today treats the Ten Commandments as if they were the ten suggestions. Never compromise on right or wrong.
-- Former college baseball coach Gordie Gillespie

God's list is a set of instructions on how you are to conduct yourself with other people and with him.

DAY 74

WATER POWER

Read Acts 10:34-48.

"Can anyone keep these people from being baptized with water? They have received the Holy Spirit just as we have" (v. 47).

Colt McCoy and his dad decided to go for a little swim across a lake, but not just for the fun of it. They went to help save a life.

McCoy, as any Longhorn football fan can tell you, won more games (45) than any other quarterback in college football history. As a senior in 2009, he won 13 of the 15 major college awards he was eligible for. His junior season he was the runner-up for the Heisman Trophy. That same season he set an all-time NCAA college football record by completing 76.7 percent of his passes. McCoy is the only quarterback in NCAA history to lead a team to ten wins per season for four seasons.

Memorial Day weekend in 2006, though, all of that success still lay ahead of the Texas freshman as he relaxed and fished with his dad, Brad, at Timber Ridge Lake. Across the way, as the day came to an end, Ken Harrington, who had worked with NASA on the first manned flight to the moon, experienced a sudden seizure. His wife screamed for help, but nobody seemed to hear.

The McCoy men did. "I looked at Colt and we could tell right away somebody was in real trouble," said Brad. "It was too far around the lake, and we didn't have a boat. We were in shorts and we looked at each other and said, 'We've got to swim.'"

So they swam across the lake, which was about 300 yards wide. When they arrived, help was on the way, but somebody had to climb the rocks to the road that lay above the lake. No one was in any kind of shape to make that climb -- except for Colt. Without any shoes and armed with a flashlight, he climbed to the road, flagged down the paramedics, and led them to Ken Harrington.

In no uncertain terms, medical personnel ordered Colt and his dad not to swim back. Instead, the two swimmers hitched a ride back to the supper they had left waiting and ready.

Children's wading pools and swimming pools in the backyard. Fishing, boating, skiing, and swimming at a lake such as Timber Ridge. Sun, sand, and surf at the beach. If there's any water around, we'll probably be in it, on it, or near it. If there's not any at hand, we'll build a dam and create our own.

We love the wet stuff for its recreational uses, but water first and foremost is about its absolute necessity to support and maintain life. From its earliest days, the Christian church appropriated water as an image for life through the ritual of baptism. Since the time of the arrival of the Holy Spirit at Pentecost, baptism with water has been the symbol of entry into the Christian community. It is water that marks a person as belonging to Jesus. It is through water that a person proclaims that Jesus is both his savior and his Lord.

There's something in the water, all right. There is life.

That's that Texas quarterback. I'm an Aggie, but I'm proud of that kid.
— A Harrington neighbor on Colt McCoy

There is life in the water:
physical life and spiritual life.

FACING THE MUSIC

Read Psalm 98.

"Sing to the Lord a new song, for he has done marvelous things" (v. 1).

A song that today is inseparable from the University of Texas first appeared as a parody.

In 1902, UT student and musician Lewis Johnson enlisted the aid of fellow student and poet John Lang Sinclair in his quest to create a song that would be the university's own. In March 1903 in the university post office, Sinclair handed Johnson a scrap of paper with a poem written on it. They set the poem to the tune of "I've Been Working on the Railroad" and then decided to revise it as a joke on university president William Prather.

Prather had attended Washington College in Virginia and had often heard its president at the time, Gen. Robert E. Lee, tell the students, "Remember, the eyes of the South are upon you." The phrase stuck with Prather, and he ended his inaugural speech in 1899 with "the eyes of Texas are upon you."

The speech was well received, so Prather concluded all of his talks with what became his catch phrase. Students being students, they picked up on it, and it soon became quite the rage to chant "Remember, the eyes of Texas are upon you" as an inside joke at just about every university function. The good-natured Prather took the ribbing as evidence the students were listening to him at least a little. This phrase was the inspiration behind the changes

Sinclair and Johnson made to the original poem.

On May 12, 1903, at a minstrel show to raise money for the track team, four students, accompanied by Sinclair on the banjo, unleashed the song "The Eyes of Texas" on the opera house packed with students. Before the first verse was over, the place was in an uproar. The audience demanded so many encores that the quartet members grew hoarse. The varsity band quickly learned the tune, and the university had a song that even today it calls its own.

Maybe you can't play a lick or carry a tune in the proverbial bucket. Or perhaps you do know your way around a guitar or a keyboard and can sing "The Eyes of Texas" on karaoke night without closing the joint down.

Unless you're a professional musician, however, how well you play or sing really doesn't matter. What counts is that you have music in your heart and sometimes you have to turn it loose.

Worshipping God has always included music in some form. That same boisterous and musical enthusiasm you exhibit when the Texas band plays "The Eyes of Texas" should be a part of the joy you have in your personal worship of God.

When you consider that God loves you, he always will, and he has arranged through Jesus for you to spend eternity with him, how can that song God put in your heart not burst forth?

Do not think you can escape them at night or early in the morn;
the Eyes of Texas are upon you til Gabriel blows his horn.
-- Lines from 'The Eyes of Texas'

You call it music; others may call it noise;
God calls it praise.

SIGHT UNSEEN

Read 2 Corinthians 5:1-10.

"We live by faith, not by sight" (v. 7).

One of the most famous catches in Texas football history was made by the receiver with his eyes closed.

The Horns were four-touchdown underdogs to Texas A&M on Thanksgiving Day 1940. The Aggies had a 19-game unbeaten streak and were the defending national champions. "I was scared to death and so was everyone else," said wingback Noble Doss about facing the Aggies. "We had a scrimmage on Tuesday, and I wouldn't have bet 25 cents on us. They had a machine."

The Horns went into the game 6-2, but they also lined up with six starters out with injuries. Coach Dana X. Bible's ranks were so thin that only thirteen players saw action. Nine of them played the full 60 minutes; the team became collectively known as "The Immortal 13."

But Bible "knew how to get an athlete's mind into thinking positive," and he had his Horns ready. On the game's first play, All-Southwest Conference fullback Pete Layden hit two-time All-American halfback Jack Crain with a 32-yard pass.

Doss then told Crain he could get behind A&M's defensive backs. The result on the fourth play of the game was The Catch, "the most famous reception in Longhorn history for almost three decades." Doss made "a twisting, over-the-head catch that carried to the Aggie one-yard line. Layden scored on the next play, Crain kicked the extra point, and 57 seconds into the game, Texas led 7-0.

That was the final score as the Immortal 13 pinned "a crushing 7-0 defeat [on] perhaps the greatest team in Aggie history."

The Catch was remarkable enough, but there was more to it than that. A famous photograph showed just what end Wally Scott claimed from the first: that Doss made the catch with his eyes closed.

To close our eyes or to be engulfed suddenly by total darkness plunges us into a world in which we struggle to function. Our world and our place in it are built on our eyesight, so much so that we tout "Seeing is believing." If we can't see it, we don't believe it. Perhaps the most famous proponent of this attitude was the disciple Thomas, who refused to believe Jesus had risen from the dead until he saw the proof for himself.

Our sight carries us only so far, however; its usefulness is restricted to the physical world. Eyesight has no place at all in spiritual matters. We don't "see" God; we don't "see" Jesus; we don't "see" God at work in the physical world. Yet we know God; we know Jesus; we know God is in control. We "know" all that because as the children of God, we live by faith and not by sight.

When we look through the eyes of faith, we understand that believing is seeing.

Look at the picture in the T Room in Memorial Stadium. I can promise you [Doss'] eyes were shut.
-- End and 1942 team captain Wally Scott on The Catch

In God's physical world, seeing is believing;
in God's spiritual world, believing is seeing.

YOU DECIDE

Read John 6:60-69.

"The words I have spoken to you are spirit and they are life. Yet there are some of you who do not believe" (vv. 63b-64a).

Darrell Royal had a decision to make, two actually: Whether to gamble and then what play to run. The only thing that hinged on his decision was the national championship.

In the 1970 Cotton Bowl, the top-ranked Horns trailed ninth-ranked Notre Dame 17-14 with only 2:26 to play. They were parked at the Irish 10 but faced a fourth-and-two. Royal called a time out, and quarterback James Street trotted over for a conference.

The options were clear and stark. The Longhorns could kick a field goal for the tie. That decision would ultimately have tossed the national championship to either Penn State or USC. Or they could risk losing the game by going for the first down.

The Irish coaches figured they knew what was coming and instructed their defense to play the run first. On the field, wide receiver Cotton Speyrer saw the defense and signaled to Royal that his defender was playing him tight and to the inside. With that information, Royal immediately made his decision: As he had done against Arkansas in the 15-14 classic a month earlier, at a time of greatest stress, he called for a pass.

"Watch for the keep[er] first," Royal instructed Street. "Drill it to Cotton. He says he's open on the out." In the huddle, Street looked right at Speyrer when he made the call. Despite being pressured, Street got off a pass; it was low but Speyrer went down and got it for the first down. Three plays later, junior halfback Billy Dale followed blocks from fullback Steve Worster and tight end Randy Peschel into the end zone.

The Horns won the game 21-17 and were unanimously voted the national champions. As it turned out, the head Longhorn had made a couple of very good decisions.

The decisions you have made along the way have shaped your life at every pivotal moment. Some decisions you made suddenly and carelessly; some you made carefully and deliberately; some were forced upon you. You may have discovered that some of those spur-of-the-moment decisions have turned out better than your carefully considered ones.

Of all your life's decisions, however, none is more important than one you cannot ignore: What have you done with Jesus? Even in his time, people chose to follow Jesus or to reject him, and nothing has changed; the decision must still be made and nobody can make it for you. Ignoring Jesus won't work either; that is, in fact, a decision, and neither he nor the consequences of your decision will go away.

Carefully considered or spontaneous -- how you reach a decision for Jesus doesn't matter; what matters is that you get there.

When you're Number 1, you've got to try to stay that way or get carried out feet first.
*   -- Darrell Royal, whose Horns stayed No. 1 by not going for the tie*

A decision for Jesus may be spontaneous or considered; what counts is that you make it.

TOP SECRET

Read Romans 2:1-16.

*"This will take place on the day when God will judge
men's secrets through Jesus Christ, as my gospel declares"
(v. 16).*

As the 1968 football season neared, the Longhorns shrouded their new offense in absolute secrecy. It turned out, though, that some students, broadcasters, and even the opposing coaches from Houston knew all about this secret.

The scheme was the brainchild of assistant coach Emory Bellard. (See Devotion No. 30.) Everything about this new-fangled formation was top secret. Darrell Royal and his coaches talked to no one about it and closed all practices to outsiders.

Then at a press party the night before the season-opening game with 11th-ranked Houston, a member of the Cougar radio broadcasting team walked up to Royal with a diagram of the new offense. He asked the coach what he called it. An understandably upset Royal asked him how he knew about it. It turned out the secret was no secret at all -- at least not in Houston.

The weak spot in the coaches' attempts at stealth lay in the fact that they obviously had to let their players in on the secret. The sister of one of the Houston players had a boyfriend who played for Texas. That Longhorn player told his girlfriend who told her brother who told his coaches that Texas had a new offense that looked a lot like the old Veer offense Houston head coach Bill Yeoman had invented in 1964.

Perhaps adding insult to injury, a Houston sportswriter was the one who came up with the name for the offense that stuck. At a press conference after the game, a 20-20 tie, a writer asked Royal what he called his offense. The head Longhorn replied, "I don't know. What do you guys think?" A writer said it looked like a chicken pully-bone and offered the name "wishbone."

Soon the whole college football world would know about this "secret" offense that took the Horns to thirty straight wins and two national titles.

We must be ever vigilant about the personal information we prefer to keep secret. Much information about us -- from credit reports to what movies we rent -- is readily available to prying and persistent persons. In our information age, people we don't know may know a lot about us — or at least they can find out.

While diligence may allow us to be reasonably successful in keeping some secrets from the world at large, we should never deceive ourselves into believing we are keeping secrets from God. God knows everything about us, including all those things we wouldn't want proclaimed at church. All our sins, mistakes, failures, shortcomings, quirks, prejudices, and desires – God knows all our would-be secrets.

But here's something God hasn't kept a secret: No matter what he knows about us, he loves us still.

In the Wishbone, all you had to do was be a little afraid.
— James Street on the secret to being a successful Wishbone quarterback

We have no secrets before God, and it's no secret
that he nevertheless loves us still.

UNBELIEVABLE!

Read Hebrews 3:7-19.

"See to it, brothers, that none of you has a sinful, unbelieving heart that turns away from the living God" (v. 12).

The 3-2 score is so pedestrian -- but the game itself and what Austin Wood did in it are simply unbelievable.

On Saturday, May 30, 2009, and Sunday, May 31, 2009, Texas and Boston College played the longest game in college baseball history. The contest in the Austin Regional required 25 innings and slightly more than seven hours -- both NCAA records -- to decide a winner. At one stretch, neither team scored a run for 18 innings. The teams set NCAA records with 42 strikeouts, 222 fielding chances, 69 assists, 192 plate appearances, and 171 official at-bats. Longhorn first baseman Preston Clark had 33 putouts, a record. Senior second baseman Travis Tucker and senior infielder Michal Torres set an NCAA record with twelve at-bats.

The winning run finally scored when Tucker slapped a single into right field that scored sophomore outfielder Connor Rowe. Freshman Austin Dicharry got the three outs in the bottom of the inning to end it, the last pitch no. 684 of the game.

And then there's what Wood did. "In my 41 years of coaching, the effort by Austin Wood was the best pitching performance I've ever seen." So declared Texas head coach Augie Garrido.

The senior lefthander who had never thrown a complete game

pitched 13 innings. For twelve and one-third of those innings he did not give up a hit. He threw 169 pitches, faced 46 batters, and ultimately give up only two hits. From the ninth inning until Dicharry relieved him in the 20th inning, every time he took the mound it was sudden death for the Longhorns.

Given Wood's unbelievable performance in this unbelievable game, he quite believably was named the regional MVP.

Much of what taxes the limits of our belief system has little direct effect on our lives. Maybe we don't believe in UFOs, honest politicians, aluminum baseball bats, Sasquatch, or the viability of electric cars. A healthy dose of skepticism is a natural defense mechanism that helps protect us in a world that all too often has designs on taking advantage of us.

That's not the case, however, when Jesus and God are part of the mix. Quite unbelievably, we often hear people blithely assert they don't believe in God. Or brazenly declare they believe in God but don't believe Jesus was anything but a good man and a great teacher.

At this point, unbelief becomes downright dangerous because God doesn't fool around with scoffers. He locks them out of the Promised Land, which isn't a country in the Middle East but is Heaven itself.

Given that scenario, it's unbelievable that anyone would not believe.

This was truly a once-in-a-lifetime experience.
-- Texas fan who sat through all 25 innings

Perhaps nothing is as unbelievable as that some people insist on not believing in God or his son.

TEXAS

DAY 80

UNEXPECTEDLY

Read Matthew 24:36-51.

"No one knows about that day or hour, not even the angels in heaven, nor the Son, but only the Father" (v. 36).

They were called "a third-rate team" that didn't belong in a bowl game. On top of that, the players didn't even want to go to a bowl. So everyone knew what to expect from the Longhorns in the 1949 Orange Bowl. Funny thing about that.

Sportswriters openly called Blair Cherry's 6-3-1 Longhorns of 1948 third-rate. They ridiculed the Orange Bowl for picking Texas in an age when what few bowls there were featured only the best teams in the country.

When Cherry brought up the Orange Bowl to his team, some of the players revolted. "About seven or eight of us seniors were married," recalled end Ralph "Peppy" Blount. "We didn't want to stay at an empty campus over the holidays when our wives had gone home." Athletic director Dana X. Bible promised to fly the players' wives to Miami and to throw in a trip to Havana for everyone. Dutifully bribed, the players agreed to play the game.

The opponent was the Georgia Bulldogs, the SEC champs. UGA quarterback Johnny Rauch knew what to expect from the game. He predicted Georgia would set an Orange Bowl scoring record.

Then the teams kicked off -- and nothing went as everyone had expected. Georgia was helpless before the Texas rushing attack; the Horns outgained UGA 332-56 on the ground. Still, Georgia led 28-27 with only five minutes left to play. But then Randall Clay scored a pair of touchdowns, and the Longhorns pulled off an unexpected 41-28 win.

Blount agreed that Rauch had been right after all; Georgia had set a scoring record. "They scored the most points for a losing team in Orange Bowl history," he pointed out.

Just like the writers covering the 1949 Orange Bowl, we think we've got everything figured out and under control, and then something unexpected happens. About the only thing we can expect from life with any certainty is the unexpected.

God is that way too, suddenly showing up to remind us he's still around. A friend who calls and tells you he's praying for you, a hug from your child or grandchild, a lone lily that blooms in your yard -- unexpected moments when the divine comes crashing into our lives with such clarity that it takes our breath away and brings tears to our eyes.

But why shouldn't God do the unexpected? The only factor limiting what God can do in our lives is the paucity of our own faith. We should as a matter of routine expect the unexpected from God, this same deity who caught everyone by surprise by unexpectedly coming to live among us as a man, and who will return when we least expect it.

The next time you writers call a team third-rate, you're going to have to play them yourselves.
-- Georgia coach Wally Butts to reporters after the 1949 Orange Bowl

God continually does the unexpected,
like showing up as Jesus,
who will return unexpectedly.

THE GOOD OLD DAYS

Read Psalm 102.

*"My days vanish like smoke; . . . but you remain the same,
and your years will never end" (vv. 3, 27).*

Homemade uniforms. A budget of $100. The players paying their own travel expenses, including gasoline and lodging. Those were the "good old days" of women's basketball at UT.

For some forty years, female athletes at Texas had maintained a tradition "of mild inquiry, complaint and protest over the lack of a real [women's basketball] team." In 1966, freshman Mary Neikirk circulated a petition that called for something more than intramural basketball and then presented it to the directors of women's PE and intramurals. They agreed to make basketball a nonvarsity club sport for the coeds.

June Walker, a member of the PE faculty, agreed to coach the new team, without any extra compensation of course. In October 1966, she held tryouts, and eleven aspirants -- including Neikirk -- made the team. Twice a week they practiced a version of the game vastly different from today's exciting sport. Each team had six players, only two of whom, the rovers, were allowed to cross the midcourt line.

In those "good old days," the women played for nothing more than love of the game, for they were ignored by the press and the public and received little support from the school. Walker's total budget the first season (1967) was $100. Home games were played on an undersized court in the Women's Gym that was not designed to accommodate spectators. The players of 1967 made their own uniforms. When they did get uniforms, they shared them with the volleyball team. They paid for their own transportation and piled into cars owned by a player or borrowed from somebody's friend.

Compared to women's basketball at UT today, maybe those "good old days" weren't so good after all.

It's a brutal truth that time just never stands still. The current of your life sweeps you along until you realize one day you've lived long enough to have a past. Part of it you cling to fondly. The stunts you pulled with your high-school buddies. Your first apartment. That dance with your first love. That special vacation. Those "good old days."

You hold on relentlessly to the memory of those old, familiar ways because of the stability they provide in our uncertain world. They will always be there even as times change and you age.

Another constant exists in your life too. God has been a part of every event in your life that created a memory because he was there. He's always there with you; the question is whether you ignore him or make him a part of your day.

A "good old day" is any day shared with God.

The players were just in a daze. I would tell them something and look them straight in the eye, and they wouldn't hear it.
-- UT women's basketball coach Rodney Page on his players' reaction to real live spectators at a game in 1974

**Today is one of the "good old days"
if you share it with God.**

RESPECTFULLY YOURS

Read Mark 8:31-38.

*"He then began to teach them that the Son of Man must
suffer many things and be rejected by the elders, chief
priests and teachers of the law, and that he must be killed"
(v. 31).*

The hype leading up to the 2006 Rose Bowl wasn't about how
this would be one of the greatest games ever played between two
sensational teams. Instead, giving the Horns little respect, the
pundits were poised for a USC coronation.

"We didn't get much respect from the media on both sides of
the ball," said Texas quarterback Vince Young about all the talk
before the game. In the weeks leading up to the Jan. 4 contest, the
Horns "heard anyone with a microphone and a can of hairspray
yammer about how USC was one of the greatest teams in college
football history."

Leading up to the game, ESPN presented a series that compared
the Trojans -- favorably, of course -- to some of the greatest teams
in college football history. And the Horns? "When the clock
struck midnight, the burnt-orange challengers would turn back
into pumpkins."

But Texas head coach Mack Brown had a different perspective
on the game. He told his team, "We don't have to be the greatest
team of all time. Just the greatest team (in the title game)."

And they were. With Young rolling up 467 all-purpose yards,

scoring three touchdowns in the last half, and winning the MVP for the second straight year, the Horns prevailed 41-38 in what Brown told USC quarterback Matt Leinart was "a classic game."

Gone was USC's 34-game win streak. Gone was USC's goal of winning a third straight national title. Gone was the coronation of the Trojans for their greatness.

In their place were the Texas Longhorns -- with their newfound and hard-earned respect as college football's national champions.

Rodney Dangerfield made a good living as a comedian with a repertoire that was basically only countless variations on one punch line: "I don't get no respect." Dangerfield was successful because he struck a chord with his audience. For instance, we all want our football team to be respected. Personally, You want the respect, the esteem, and the regard that you feel you've earned.

But more often than not, you don't get it. Still, you shouldn't feel too badly; you're in good company. In the ultimate example of disrespect, Jesus – the very Son of God -- was treated as the worst type of criminal. He was arrested, bound, scorned, ridiculed, spit upon, tortured, condemned, and executed.

God allowed his son to undergo such treatment because of his high regard and his love for you. You are respected by almighty God! Could anyone else's respect really matter?

If you have to hand it over and step aside for somebody, that's a heck of a team to do that for.
-- USC coach Pete Carroll, giving the Horns their due

**You may not get the respect you deserve,
but at least nobody's spitting on you
and driving nails into you as they did to Jesus.**

ON THE MONEY

Read Luke 16:1-15.

"You cannot serve both God and money" (v. 13b).

Today's NFL draft amounts to the overnight creation of multi-millionaires. As Hugh Wolfe knew from experience, though, it wasn't always that way.

Wolfe was the first Longhorn ever taken in the NFL draft. He came to the University in 1933 and left as one of the greatest athletes of his age. He earned five letters in football and track and field, was twice an All-Southwest Conference fullback, was second-team All-America in 1937, and won the conference discus title. On the track and field team, in addition to throwing the discus, he ran the 100-yard and 440-yard dashes, high jumped, and pole vaulted. He spent five years at Texas because he missed the '35 season after eye surgery.

Wolfe had the game's longest run in the 7-6 win over Notre Dame in 1934, the first time in history the Irish had lost a season-opening home game. In a loss to top-ranked Minnesota in 1936, he quick-kicked 90 yards and set a school record with a 95-yard kickoff return for a touchdown. In the game's most bizarre play, he hit an onside kickoff that kept rolling until it wound up in the end zone and was recovered by a teammate for a touchdown. His 38-yard field goal beat Baylor 9-6 in '34, knocking the Bears out of the Rose Bowl.

Like many other students during some tough economic times,

LONGHORNS

Wolfe struggled financially. "I don't know how I got by," he once said. "But I managed some way." He managed mostly by mopping floors and, as he called it, "hustling" his room and board. He also swept out Gregory Gym each day for 50 cents an hour.

The Pittsburgh Steelers drafted him in 1938, but he was traded right away to the New York Giants. He received no signing bonus, and his first contract was for $4,000. Wolfe signed it without even reading it because "that was a lot of money, then." But it wasn't anything like what today's instant millionaires receive.

Having a little too much money at the end of the month may be as bothersome -- if not as worrisome -- as having a little too much month at the end of the money. The investment possibilities are bewildering: stocks, bonds, mutual funds, joining a group to open up a neighborhood coffee shop -- that's a good idea.

You take your money seriously, as well you should. Jesus, too, took money seriously, warning us frequently of its dangers. Money itself is not evil; its peril lies in the ease with which it can usurp God's rightful place as the master of our lives.

Certainly in our age and society, we often measure people by how much money they have. But like our other talents, gifts, and resources, money should primarily be used for God's purposes. God's love must touch not only our hearts but our wallets also.

How much of your wealth are you investing with God?

Money can buy you everything but happiness. It can pay your fare to everywhere but heaven.

-- *Pete Maravich*

**Your attitude about money says much
about your attitude toward God.**

REST EASY

Read Hebrews 4:1-11.

*"There remains, then, a Sabbath rest for the people of God;
for anyone who enters God's rest also rests from his own
work, just as God did from his. Let us, therefore, make
every effort to enter that rest" (vv. 9-11).*

Rick Barnes realized what kind of chore he had in front of him
when, during his first day on the job, a player told him the off-
season was their time, not his.

Barnes took over the Texas men's basketball program in 1998.
Through the 2013-14 season, he had coached the Longhorns to
sixteen NCAA appearances (including fifteen in a row) and fifteen 20-win seasons, fourteen in a row at one stretch.

That first day on the job, he met with his veteran players. That's
when he met an attitude that left him "thunderstruck," the idea
the players held that college basketball included a long off-season.
Barnes didn't know whether to laugh or to cry. What he did know
was that he had to change the players' mindset right away if Texas
was to win. They had to buy totally into the notion that college
basketball offered no one a break.

Fortunately for the history of the program, they did. In the
summer of 2000, freshman guard Darren Kelly declared, "Even
when I don't have to be, I'm in a gym, playing. You can't get tired
of it." Another freshman guard, Brandon Mouton, agreed, saying,
"I don't think a day goes by that I don't pick up a basketball."

Chris Ogden, a sophomore forward at the time, observed that some players at other schools did take time off. "One thing I've noticed when I talk to those guys," he said. "They all play on the last-place teams in our league." In other words, they got a break while the Horns were playing in the NCAA Tournament.

Like the Longhorn basketball players, you don't have an off-season in your life. That doesn't mean, however, that you don't have some down time. As part of the natural rhythm of life, rest is important to maintain physical health. Rest has different images, though: a good eight hours in the sack; a Saturday morning that begins in the backyard with the paper and a pot of coffee; a vacation in the mountains, where the most strenuous thing you do is change position in the hot tub.

Rest is also part of the rhythm and the health of our spiritual lives. Often we envision the faithful person as someone who is always busy, always doing something for God whether it's teaching Sunday school or showing up at church every time the doors open.

But God himself rested from work, and in blessing us with the Sabbath, he calls us into a time of rest. To rest by simply spending time in the presence of God is to receive spiritual revitalization and rejuvenation. Sleep refreshes your body and your mind; God's rest refreshes your soul.

If you want to be good, you don't sit around and twiddle your thumbs. You've got to get out and go.
— Rick Barnes saying there's no break in basketball

**God promises you a spiritual rest
that renews and refreshes your soul.**

WEATHERPROOFED

Read Nahum 1:3-9.

"His way is in the whirlwind and the storm, and clouds are the dust of his feet" (v. 3b).

The Horns made history when they played Missouri on Aug. 31, 1996, but so did the weather.

The occasion was the beginning of a new era in college football, the first-ever Big 12 game. It wasn't just the conference that was new that night. Texas' "maiden voyage into the Big 12" included a new grass field, a new scoreboard, a new Jumbotron television screen, and a new name for the stadium. On this history-making night, sophomore Ricky Williams rambled for 112 yards and two touchdowns to lead the Horns to a 40-10 pasting of the Tigers.

History was made on another front that night. In its 72 seasons, Memorial Stadium had never had a rain delay. In its first-ever game, the newly christened Royal-Memorial Stadium had one. The Horns expected their usual home-field advantage from the heat and the humidity, but they got a surprise with "a thunderstorm that would have sent Noah scrambling for his deck shoes."

Texas led 20-10 when the two teams trotted out to start the last half and were greeted by forty mph winds and nearby lightning flashes. As Missouri snapped the ball for the half's second play, the heavens opened up and delivered a torrential rainstorm that before it exhausted itself 25 minutes later dumped two inches of rain on the field. Thus drenched, the Tigers promptly had two false starts, mishandled a pitch, and lofted a 10-yard punt. The Horns quickly moved in for the kill with Williams scoring on a 12-yard touchdown run that made it 27-10 with 7:59 on the clock.

And that's when more history was made. The refs decided the lightning was now a real threat and called the teams off the field. The first home rain delay in UT football history ensued, lasting 45 minutes. One wag said the evening amounted to a "Royal flush."

A thunderstorm washes away your golf game or the family picnic. Lightning knocks out the electricity just as you settle in at the computer for some work. A tornado interrupts your Sunday dinner and sends everyone scurrying for shelter. A hurricane blows away your vacation.

For all our technology and our knowledge, we are still at the mercy of the weather, able only to get a little more advance warning than in the past. That's because the weather doesn't answer to us; it answers only to God. Rain and hail will fall where they want to; the weather will be totally inconsiderate of something as important as a Texas football game.

We stand mute before the awesome power of the weather, but we should be even more awestruck at the power of the one who controls it, a power beyond our imagining. Neither, however, can we imagine the depths of God's love for us, a love that drove him to die on a cross for us.

The wind started howling. Then we looked behind us and saw lightning.
-- UT fan on the weather at the '96 Missouri game

The power of the one who controls the weather
is beyond anything we can imagine,
but so is his love for us.

THE PIONEER SPIRIT

Read Luke 5:1-11.

"So they pulled their boats up on shore, left everything and followed him" (v. 11).

They had no background in their sport, most of them selected for it because they appeared tall and strong. One played a flute in high school and was not an athlete. Yet, they were the pioneers of a Longhorn sport that from its inception dominated the Big 12.

The University of Texas started a women's rowing program in 1998 as part of a lawsuit settlement that mandated an increase in women's sports at the school. Carie Graves, who had won a gold medal at the 1984 Olympics and had coached at both Harvard and Northeastern, was hired as the head coach.

The first problem Graves had was coming up with some rowers, which meant putting up flyers, stuffing brochures into orientation packets for new students, and scouring the campus, on the prowl for tall women with athletic builds. "It's a time-honored tradition" in rowing, the coach said. Assistant coach Caroline King hung out at busy spots around campus, looking for the students who fit the bill. "We really just kind of hunt people down," she said.

The result was pioneers like Kate Ronkainen, who had played basketball in high school. "I didn't even know what rowing was, but I thought, 'That sounds cool,'" she said. She eventually was good enough to land a spot on the U.S. national team. The only thing Mary Beth Goodnight had played in high school was a flute.

She heard about UT rowing when a customer at a clothing store where she worked suggested she give it a try. She did and, much to her surprise, made the varsity.

They and other "young women who didn't even know what the sport was" were the pioneers who launched a program that won seven consecutive Big 12 Invitationals and then won the first three conference championships from 2009-11.

Going to a place in your life you've never been before requires a willingness to take risks and face uncertainty head-on. You may have never helped start a new sports program at a major college, but you've had your moments when your latent pioneer spirit manifested itself. That time you changed careers, volunteered at a homeless shelter, learned Spanish, or went back to school.

While attempting new things invariably begets apprehension, the truth is that when life becomes too comfortable and too familiar, it gets boring. The same is true of God, who is downright dangerous because he calls us to be anything but comfortable as we serve him. He summons us to continuously blaze new trails in our faith life, to follow him no matter what.

Stepping out on faith is risky all right, but the reward is a life of accomplishment, adventure, and joy that cannot be equaled anywhere else.

I'm making something of my life. I'm an NCAA athlete and I never thought I'd be able to do anything like that.
-- UT pioneer rower Mary Beth Goodnight

Unsafe and downright dangerous, God calls us out of the place where we are comfortable to a life of adventure and trailblazing in his name.

HAVE COURAGE

Read 1 Corinthians 16:13-14.

"Be on your guard; stand firm in the faith; be men of courage; be strong" (v. 13).

Mack Brown started the tradition in 1998: As the Longhorn football players trot onto the field for a game, on their way they touch a photograph of Freddie Steinmark to remind them to play with the courage that he showed in his own life.

Steinmark was a starting safety for Texas as a sophomore and as a junior in 1968-69. He snared five interceptions while the Longhorns won 20 of 22 games and two SWC championships. He led the team in punt returns in 1968 and was a significant part of the "Game of the Century," the 15-14 win over Arkansas that propelled the undefeated Horns to the 1969 national championship.

Steinmark had played for some time with a nagging pain in his left thigh, and when he visited the team doctor the Monday after the Arkansas win, the diagnosis was swift, sure, and devastating: He had bone cancer. Less than a week after the Arkansas game, Steinmark's leg was amputated. The safety's courage and attitude drew national attention. President Richard Nixon phoned after the surgery for an update. More than 10,000 Arkansas fans sent get-well wishes. Texas A&M wired a telegram 60 feet long.

Less than a month after his surgery, Steinmark amazed his doctors and his teammates by showing up in the locker room for the Cotton Bowl against Notre Dame. "It was like the old Freddie," said quarterback James Street. After Texas won 21-17, coach Darrell Royal gave Steinmark both an emotional hug on the sideline and the game ball in the dressing room.

Steinmark served as an assistant coach for the freshman team his senior season, but his cancer spread. He died on June 6, 1971, courageous, upbeat, and fighting until the end; he was 22.

When we speak of courage, we often think of heroic actions such as those displayed by soldiers during wartime or firefighters during an inferno. But as Freddie Steinmark's life demonstrates, there is another aspect to courage.

Freddie Steinmark certainly was afraid during the last years of his life. What made his daily life courageous and admirable was not the absence of fear, which often results from foolhardiness or a dearth of relevant information. Rather, his courage showed itself in his determined refusal to let fear debilitate him.

This is the courage God calls upon us to demonstrate in our faith lives. When Paul urged the Christians in Corinth to "be men of courage," he wasn't telling them to rush into burning buildings. He was admonishing them to be strong and sure in their faith in Jesus Christ.

This courageous attitude is an absolute necessity for American Christians today when our faith is under attack as never before. Our courage reveals itself in our proclaiming the name of Jesus, no matter what forces are arrayed against us.

Mother, if God wants my leg, we'll have to give it to Him.
-- Freddie Steinmark as he went in for surgery

To be courageous for Jesus is to speak his name
no matter what tactics Satan uses against us.

ON THE JOB

Read Acts 9:1-21.

"'This man is my chosen instrument to carry my name before the Gentiles and their kings and before the people of Israel'" (v. 15).

If it had to do with athletics at the University of Texas, Clyde Littlefield was the right man for the job.

Littlefield was once called "Texas's answer to Jim Thorpe and Bo Jackson." The difference was he didn't leave his mark in baseball. He did pitch two games and bat 1.000 in a brief fling with the Longhorn baseball team, but he gave the sport up. Not because he couldn't excel at it, but because he didn't have enough time for it. Littlefield was too busy earning twelve letters at Texas in basketball, track, and football from 1912-16.

In football, Littlefield "was the right man for times that were changing." Dramatic rules changes in 1912 opened up the passing game, which played right into Littlefield's skills. He could throw the ball sixty yards with accuracy, a feat virtually unmatched in those days of the rounder ball. In a 92-0 blowout of Daniel Baker in 1915, he threw four touchdown passes of 33 yards or more and ran for three more.

Littlefield was Texas' first-ever basketball All-America, leading the undefeated squad of 1915 in scoring. (He also led the football team in scoring that season.) He was called "the key figure" in three straight undefeated seasons. (See Devotion No. 94.)

LONGHORNS

In track, his specialty was the 120-yard high hurdles. He lost only one race in college and tied the world record in 1914.

The Horns hired him in 1920 to head up the track program. (He also coached freshman football and basketball and taught PE.) He coached track and field for 41 years; his teams won 25 conference titles. From 1927-33, Littlefield was the head football coach, winning conference titles in 1928 and 1930. In 1927 and '28, his Horns shut out ten opponents in a row.

Clyde Littlefield was the right man for the job -- whatever it was.

What do you want to be when you grow up? Somehow you are supposed to know the answer to that question when you're a teenager, the time in life when common sense and logic are at their lowest ebb. Long after those halcyon teen years are left behind, you may make frequent career changes. You chase the job that gives you not just financial rewards but also some personal satisfaction and sense of accomplishment. You desire a profession that uses your abilities, that you enjoy doing, and that gives you a sense of contributing to something bigger than yourself.

God, too, wants you in the right job, one that he has designed specifically for you. After all, even Saul, a renowned persecutor of Christians, was the right man for what God needed done. To do his work, God gave you abilities, talents, and passions. Do what you do best and what you love -- just do it for God's glory.

The price of success is hard work and dedication to the job at hand.
-- Vince Lombardi

God has a job for you, one for which he gave you particular talents, abilities, and passions.

THE CHALLENGE

Read Matthew 4:12-25.

"Come, follow me," Jesus said (v. 19).

When the challenger meets the champion, and the challenger wins, there is a new champion." With those words on national television prior to the 1964 Cotton Bowl, the head coach of second-ranked Navy threw a challenge right into the face of Darrell Royal and his top-ranked Longhorns.

The Horns of 2004 knew exactly how their 1964 counterparts felt as they prepared to take on Texas Tech on Oct. 23. Though it was Texas who was ranked 8th in the nation, everyone was talking about the Red Raiders. The so-called experts even established them as one-point favorites. They predicted a Tech win. Raider fans were confident, perhaps even cocky, while Longhorn fans were "at best apprehensive."

Not the Texas players and coaches, though. They weren't interested in talking big and offering up challenges; they were quietly going about the business of preparing to win the game. Greg Robinson, Duane Akina, Dick Tomey, and Mike Tolleson -- the defensive brain trust -- "were actually having fun" as they prepared for a Raider offense that had hung 70 points on Nebraska the week before. "Some folks fear a challenge; these guys relished it."

What resulted was "the most complete victory over a very good football team by a Longhorn squad in a long, long time." Texas slaughtered Tech 51-21. Twenty seconds into the fourth quarter,

Tech could have held the ball for the remainder of the game and still lost the time of possession, so complete was the Longhorn dominance.

The Horns had met the challenge.

And by the way, what was Darrell Royal's response to the challenge thrown at him back in '64 right before Texas shellacked Navy 28-6? He said what turned out to be two, very true words: "We're ready."

Like the Texas Longhorn athletic teams every time they take the field or the court, we are challenged daily. Life is a testing ground; God intentionally set it up that way. If we are to grow in character, confidence, and perseverance, and if we are to make a difference in the world, we must meet challenges head-on. Few things in life are as boring and as destructive to our sense of self-worth as a job that doesn't offer any challenges.

Our faith life is the same way. The moment we answered Jesus' call to "Come, follow me," we took on the most difficult challenge we will ever face. We are called to be holy by walking in Jesus' footsteps in a world that seeks to render our Lord irrelevant and his influence negligible. The challenge Jesus places before us is to put our faith and our trust in him and not in ourselves or the transitory values of the secular world.

Daily walking in Jesus' footsteps is a challenge, but the path takes us all the way to Heaven's gates – and right on through.

Sports challenge you and build character for everything you do in life.
-- Howie Long

To accept Jesus as Lord is to joyfully take on the challenge of living a holy life in an unholy world.

REDEEMED

Read 1 Peter 1:17-25.

"It was not with perishable things such as silver or gold that you were redeemed from the empty way of life handed down to you from your forefathers, but with the precious blood of Christ" (vv. 18-19).

Chris Simms needed some redemption. He found it in -- of all places -- Stillwater with a record-tying performance that left the Longhorn faithful standing and cheering.

Frustrated and angry Texas fans lit up radio talk shows and flooded the Internet with calls for Simms to be benched in favor of Major Applewhite after he threw four interceptions in a 14-3 loss to Oklahoma on Oct. 6, 2001. "With everything that was on the Internet, on the radio and the paper this week, we tried to stay away from it," admitted offensive coordinator Greg Davis. "But we're not stupid." So how did Simms respond in practice to all the criticism? "He didn't sit around and mope," Davis said. "He prepared himself well this week."

Still, Simms and his team were on a mission to find redemption when they headed up the road to take on Oklahoma State the following Saturday. And, boy, did they find it.

Simms tied a school record by throwing five touchdown passes. Only seven days from leading his team to an embarrassing three points against Oklahoma, he was responsible for six touchdowns in Texas' 45-17 romp, the sixth score coming on a 1-yard run. For the game, he completed 18 of 30 passes for 235 yards. The junior signal caller had plenty of help from tailback Cedric Benson, who rushed for 131 yards in his first collegiate start.

"Of course this feels great," Simms said as he trotted off the field to the tune of a standing ovation from a large pocket of UT fans. "We needed this game really badly," Simms admitted, referring to both his team and to himself.

In our capitalistic society, we know all about redemption. Just think "rebate" or store or product coupons. To receive the rebates or the discount, though, we must redeem them, cash them in.

"Redemption" is a business term; it reconciles a debt, restoring one party to favor by making amends as was the case with Chris Simms and the Longhorns, whose game against Oklahoma State returned them to their fans' graces. In the Bible, a slave could obtain his freedom only upon the paying of money by a redeemer. In other words, redemption involves the cancelling of a debt the individual cannot pay on his own.

While literal, physical slavery is incomprehensible to us today, we nevertheless live much like slaves in our relationship to sin. On our own, we cannot escape from its consequence, which is death. We need a redeemer, someone to pay the debt that gives us the forgiveness from sin we cannot give ourselves.

We have such a redeemer. He is Jesus Christ, who paid our debt not with money, but with his own blood.

It's redemption, but at the same time, we're not going to be satisfied.
-- Chris Simms after the 2001 Oklahoma State win

To accept Jesus Christ as your savior is to believe his death was a selfless act of redemption.

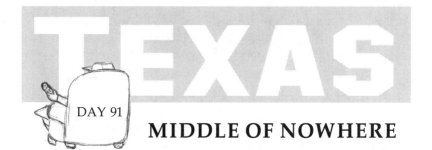

MIDDLE OF NOWHERE

Read Genesis 28:10-22.

"When Jacob awoke from his sleep, he thought, 'Surely the Lord is in this place, and I was not aware of it'" (v. 16).

A cousin had a hot tip for her coaching kin at Texas, but it came with a problem: The coach had to find the prospect.

The coach was Jody Conradt, and while the cousin's tips didn't always pan out, this one was worth a look. Even if it meant going to some place named Windthorst to see some player named Heather Schreiber.

Schreiber is part of Texas women's basketball history. A 6-2 forward, she started every game from 2001-05 (133). She received All-Big 12 honors three times and made the final list for national player of the year awards her last two seasons. For her career, she scored 1,705 points and grabbed 856 rebounds and was second all-time in school history in career free-throw percentage. Her last semester at UT, she joined the volleyball team.

And Conradt found her in a place "at least an hour's tractor drive from Wichita Falls that's so small with a population of 350 that her kinesiology class at UT [was] more than half as large." That would be Windthorst. There was no Dairy Queen there. No Wal-Mart. No stop light. A blinking light is the community's contribution to traffic control.

So where does a young girl go for fun in such a place? Schreiber knew: "The gym," she said. In that gym, she led her local high school with its full complement of 119 students to four straight volleyball state championships and a berth in the state basketball tournament. Just for good measure, she moved outdoors to win the state high jump title.

But Schreiber knew a little bit about the great outdoors. From the fourth grade on, she climbed out of bed each morning at 3 to help milk her family's 100 Holstein cows before she went to school and played some ball. There in the middle of nowhere.

Ever heard tell of Tell? Done any work in Tool? Spent the night in Sundown or passed a restful day in Placid?

They are among the many small communities, some of them nothing more than crossroads, that dot the Texas countryside. Not on any interstate highway, they seem to be in the middle of nowhere, the kind of place where Heather Schreiber could have been found growing up with a basketball in her hands. They're just hamlets we zip right on through on our way to somewhere important.

But don't be misled; those villages are indeed special and wonderful. That's because God is in Elbert and Melvin just as he is in Austin, Houston, Dallas, and San Antonio. Even when you are far off the roads well traveled, you are with God. As Jacob discovered one rather astounding morning, the middle of nowhere is, in fact, holy ground -- because God is there.

The number of people at UT. Just seeing so many people around campus. I was not used to that at all.
— Heather Schreiber on her biggest adjustment to college life

**No matter how far off the beaten path you travel,
you are still on holy ground because God is there.**

A GOOD IMPRESSION

Read John 1:1-18.

"In the beginning was the Word, and the Word was with God, and the Word was God. . . . The Word became flesh and made his dwelling among us" (vv. 1, 14).

Few players in the fabled history of Texas Longhorn football have ever made a more startling and favorable first impression than did Bobby Dillon.

As a senior, Dillon was an All-American safety for and co-captain of the 1951 Longhorns, champions of the Southwest Conference. He went on to an All-Pro career with the Green Bay Packers and is a member of the Packer, the Longhorn, and the Texas Sports halls of fame. He still owns the school record for the highest punt return average for a season (an incredible 22.3 yards per return in 1950) and a career (17.7 yards from 1949-51).

In the 1949 season opener against Texas Tech, Dillon went into the game as a second safety on a fourth-down play. But when Tech punted, what happened next amazed even Dillon himself. He caught the punt and returned it about 60 yards for a touchdown. "I was pretty amazed," Dillon confessed.

It wasn't the last time Dillon made an impression. In the 27-20 win over Baylor in 1950, he returned a punt 85 yards for the game-winning touchdown. He almost beat Oklahoma that season. With the score tied 7-7, he took an interception in for a touchdown, but Texas missed the extra point and went on to lose 14-13.

LONGHORNS

Perhaps as remarkable as Dillon's first impression and his overall talent was that he played with a handicap that today would probably keep him off the football field entirely. When he was 10, he lost his left eye after a series of accidents. Doctors replaced it with an artificial one, and he went on to play in an age that did not offer any gear to protect his good eye.

That guy in the apartment next door. A job search complete with interview. A twenty-year class reunion. The new neighbors. We are constantly about the fraught task of wanting to make an impression on people. We want them to remember us, obviously in a flattering way.

We make that impression, good or bad, generally in two ways. Even with instant communication on the Internet – perhaps especially with the Internet – we primarily influence the opinion others have of us by our words. After that, we can advance to the next level by making an impression with our actions.

Interestingly enough, God gave us an impression of himself in exactly the same way. In Jesus, God took the unprecedented step of appearing to us mortals as one of us, as mere flesh and bone. We now know the sorts of things God does and the sorts of things God says.

In Jesus, God put his divine foot forward to make a good impression on each one of us.

The first play I ever played, the first time I touched the ball, I ran for a touchdown. I think I made a pretty good impression.
-- Bobby Dillon

**Through Jesus' words and actions,
God seeks to impress us with his love.**

RUN FOR IT

Read John 20:1-10.

"Peter and the other disciple started for the tomb. Both were running, but the other disciple outran Peter and reached the tomb first" (vv. 3-4).

What made Earl Campbell run? According to Earl, the answer was pretty simple: God did.

Campbell, of course, is a Texas legend, the first Heisman Trophy winner in UT history and the player many still regard as the greatest running back in Texas high-school history. As a senior in 1977, he led the nation in rushing and points scored; the Horns of first-year coach Fred Akers went 11-0 in the regular season. Campbell was All-America both as a sophomore and a senior. A hamstring injury slowed him down in 1976. The problem was located deep within Campbell's thigh, which measured 30 inches, more than many college students' waists. Thus, trainers and doctors had trouble getting to it to treat it.

Early in his life, though, the "Tyler Rose" appeared to be running to nowhere. "I used to be a thug from about the time I was in the sixth grade until I went into high school," he admitted. "I did just about everything there was except get mixed up with drugs." But every Sunday, Campbell's mama made sure he was front and center at Hopewell Baptist No. 1. And one night Earl turned away from his street life and turned to God. "Out on the black tar road that passed by where we lived, I said, 'Lord, lift me up,'" Campbell recalled.

And, oh, how the Lord lifted him up and set him to running. Asked once what made him run, Campbell replied that running was "a part of me, just like the clothes I wear. . . . It's a gift that God gave me and this is what I am meant to do."

Each time that he sat on the sideline during a game, Campbell prepared himself to run again by praying. "People wonder how I get out there and run like I do," he said. "I sit on the bench, I put on that suit, and I say a prayer."

Hit the ground running -- every morning that's what you do as you leave the house and re-enter the rat race. You run errands; you run though a presentation; you give someone a run for his money; you always want to be in the running and never run-of-the-mill.

You're always running toward something, such as your goals, or away from something, such as your past. Many of us spend much of our lives foolhardily trying to run away from God, the purposes he has for us, and the uncountable blessings he waits to give us.

No matter how hard or how far you run, though, you can never outrun yourself or God. God keeps pace with you, calling you in the short run to take care of the long run by falling to your knees and running for your life -- to Jesus -- just as Peter and the other disciple ran that first Easter morning.

On your knees, you run all the way to glory.

Earl, when you get in that end zone, act like you have been there before.
-- Darrell Royal to Earl Campbell

You can run to eternity by going to your knees.

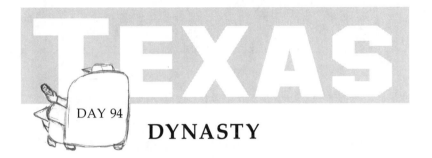

DYNASTY

Read 2 Samuel 7:8-17.

"Your house and your kingdom will endure forever before me; your throne will be established forever" (v. 16).

Through the decades, Longhorn fans have become accustomed to the perception of their football team as a dynasty, particularly within its conference. The first-ever UT dynasty, however -- one that set a winning streak the football team has never equaled -- actually belongs to the men's basketball program.

The sport began at Texas in 1905-06 but ran into some serious trouble almost as soon as it started when it lost $200 in the 1906-07 season. It survived that early fiscal problem, but the team had no gym and played its games outdoors on Clark Field, sharing the venue with football, track, and baseball.

By 1916, interest in the program was so high that construction of a new wooden gym was under way. The place was no palace; it lacked good lighting and had no heat, but it was dry. And it was home. The facility was christened on Jan. 24, 1917, with a 34-14 victory over Southwestern. For a while, the team had played its games in the Scottish Rite Theatre, renting the place for $75 a night, an arrangement that ended after the 1912-13 season.

The basketball squad won its last three games of that season. When the 1914 season began, the star of the team was Clyde Little-field. (See Devotion No. 88.) Littlefield, Pete Edmond, and Gus Dittmar, all football players, led the team to an 11-0 record. In

1915, the talented team added H.C. Blackburn, and with Littlefield averaging 19 points a game, Texas went 14-0.

The 1916 season included wins by scores of 102-1 and 80-7 as the team went undefeated for a third straight year. The first basketball dynasty in collegiate history ended in 1917 with a loss to Rice, but not until Texas had won an incredible 44 straight games.

No matter how good it is or how strong the organization that supports it, every team will inevitably lose. History teaches us that kingdoms, empires, countries, and sports programs all rise and fall. Dynasties end as events and circumstances conspire and align to snap all winning streaks.

Your life is like that; you win some and lose some. You get a promotion on Monday and then your son gets arrested on Friday. You breeze through your annual physical but your dog dies. You finally line up a date with that cutie next door and get sent out of town on business.

Only one dynasty will never end because it is based upon an everlasting promise from God. God promised David the king an enduring line in the appearance of one who would establish God's kingdom forever. That one is Jesus Christ, the reigning king of God's eternal and unending dynasty.

The only way to lose out on that one is to stand on the sidelines and not get in the game.

Dynasties, streaks, and careers all come to an end eventually.
-- ESPN's Mr. Clean

All dynasties and win streaks end except the one
God established with Jesus as its king;
this one never loses and never will.

WHOLEHEARTEDLY

Read 1 Samuel 13:1-14.

"The Lord has sought out a man after his own heart" (v. 14).

You're not even five feet tall. Soaking wet you may weigh 130 pounds. Fittingly, you're the football team's water boy. And yet you become a kicker at the University of Texas and even throw a couple of trick-play passes? How in the world? It takes heart, not size, and Billy "Rooster" Andrews had it.

At 4'10" tall, Andrews was a manager for the UT football team from 1941-45. During the 1943 season, Coach Dana X. Bible held weekly contests to find a reliable kicker. He noticed that Andrews was good at drop-kicking, which by then had pretty much passed out of vogue. Before the TCU game, Bible asked Andrews to join a kicking contest. He beat out three other players.

Andrews got his chance in the second half of the Horns' 46-7 romp past the Horned Frogs. He made two drop kicks and had a third blocked. The TCU coach was furious, accusing Bible of rubbing it in by using a water boy as a kicker. He dared Bible to use Andrews against a tough A&M team the following week. Bible didn't hesitate, and Andrews made two of three extra points in a 27-13 win.

In 1944, Bobby Layne showed up after a stint in the Merchant Marines, and the two were roommates. "They were inseparable. [Andrews] spent half his time keeping Layne out of trouble, the rest joining him." One night during the '44 season, Layne woke up his roomie with an idea. "When you're back there drop-kicking on extra points, I wonder if we could fake the thing and you could throw it to me on the left flat," he said. During a 20-0 win over Oklahoma, Layne called "our play" in the huddle. It worked then, and it worked again in the 1946 Cotton Bowl against Missouri.

Andrews was said to be second only to his roommate in popularity among the students. One of those was the woman who would become his wife of more than fifty years. She said of him, "He was such a big man on campus."

He was big right where it mattered: in the heart.

Loving and serving God is all about heart like Billy Andrews had. At some time in your life, you probably have admitted you were whipped no matter how much it hurt. Always, though, you have known that you would fight for some things with all your heart and never give them up: your family, your country, your friends, your core beliefs.

God should be on that list too. God seeks men and women who will never turn their back on him because they are people after God's own heart. That is, they will never betray God with their unbelief; they will never lose their childlike trust in God; they will never cease to love God with all their heart.

They are lifetime members of God's team; it's a mighty good one to be on, but it takes heart.

His heart is way bigger than he is.
-- Mack Brown on 'Rooster' Andrews

**To be on God's team requires
the heart of a champion.**

ON CALL

Read 1 Samuel 3:1-18.

*"The Lord came and stood there, calling as at the other
times, 'Samuel! Samuel!' Then Samuel said, 'Speak, for
your servant is listening'" (v. 10).*

Every time he got the call, he'd pump up and go out there." So
spoke Darrell Royal about Large Leo Brooks.

Brooks was indeed a large man. He stood 6-foot-6 and weighed
250 pounds in a day when the average offensive lineman topped
the scales at 210 pounds. He was also strong, one of the side
effects of working on ranches and in construction as he did. He
spent one summer while he was at UT hauling shingles in a
lumber yard and another on a construction crew that built Jester
Dormitory.

Brooks was a back-up offensive lineman in 1968. The Horns
were only one game into the legendary string of victories that
eventually would reach 30 when fate stepped in with a key move
that had a lot to do with many of those wins. Against Oklahoma,
the Horns trailed 14-6, and the Sooners were moving in for the
kill late in the first half. Two players left the game with injuries, so
in desperation defensive line coach R.M. Patterson put Brooks in.
On the first play, Brooks sacked the quarterback for a six-yard loss,
thus killing the drive. From then on, he was a defensive tackle.
UT won the game 26-20.

As a senior in 1969, Brooks was All-Southwest Conference. He went on to a Pro-Bowl career that ended when he answered the call by coming back home to Texas to run the family ranch when his father-in-law died.

Royal praised Brooks for answering the call in the Arkansas game the week after his defensive debut against Oklahoma. He made seventeen tackles and was named the conference lineman of the week in the Texas win. He played the whole game so sick he could barely breathe. "I wasn't aware he was sick until the game was under way," Royal said. "Once pretty early he came out and had a hard time breathing. He was pretty sick."

But then as always, Large Leo Brooks answered the call.

Answering the call in football means doing whatever is necessary for the good of the team. Something quite similar occurs when God places a specific call upon a Christian's life.

This is much scarier, though, than playing sick as Leo Brooks did. The way many folks understand it is that answering God's call means going into the ministry, packing the family up, and moving halfway around the world to some place where folks have never heard of air conditioning, fried chicken, paved roads, or the Longhorns. Zambia. The Philippines. Cleveland even.

Not for you, no thank you. And who can blame you?

But God usually calls folks to serve him where they are. In fact, God put you where you are right now, and he has a purpose in placing you there. Wherever you are, you are called to serve him.

Leo Brooks is trustworthy. He gives a good effort all the time.
— Darrell Royal

God calls you to serve him right now
right where he has put you, wherever that is.

BELIEVE IT

Read John 3:16-21.

"For God so loved the world that He gave His only begotten Son, that whoever believes in Him should not perish but have everlasting life" (v. 16 NKJV).

When the 7-2 Horns left for Stillwater for the game of Nov. 3, 2007, each of them carried a folded cardboard itinerary with "We believe" on the front. As the fourth quarter ticked relentlessly away, though, that belief was being sorely tested.

The Oklahoma State Cowboys jumped out to a 21-0 lead, withstood a Texas rally, and then regained the big lead at 35-14 as the fourth quarter rolled on. On fourth and three at the Texas 35, the Cowboys went for it, and cornerback Deon Beasley stopped an end-around for a six-yard loss. The Longhorn offense responded by quickly moving 59 yards, sophomore tailback Jamaal Charles covering the last 18. It was 35-21 with 11:40 left in the game.

Beasley broke up a pass on third down to force an OSU punt. The kick was downed at the 1-yard line, leaving the Horns behind by 14 with only 9:01 to play and 99 yards to navigate. "Visions of their South Division showdown with Oklahoma . . . had to be dancing in the heads of the faithful in Stillwater."

The Horns moved out to the 25 where, suddenly, Charles got a block, found a hole, and went 75 yards with 7:30 left. It was 35-28. The Longhorn faithful began to believe again.

The Horn defense forced another punt, this one backing Texas up to its own 9. Again, the Horns moved the ball, and from the 30, Colt McCoy hit wide-out Jordan Shipley in stride. He was pulled down at the Cowboy 1. Vondrell McGee got the last yard with 3:22 to play. It was 35-35, and faith was alive and well in Austin.

Texas got the ball back with 1:13 to play. McCoy led a brilliant drive, and with two seconds on the clock, Ryan Bailey booted a 40-yard field goal. Even though many shellshocked OSU fans couldn't believe it, Texas had a 38-35 win.

What we believe underscores everything about our lives. Our politics. How we raise our children. How we treat other people. Whether we respect others, their property and their lives.

Often, competing belief systems clamor for our attention; we all know persons who have lost Christianity in the shuffle and the hubbub. We turn aside from believing in Christ at our peril, however, because the heart and soul, the very essence of Christianity, is belief. That is, believing that this man named Jesus is the very Son of God and that it is through him – and only through him – that we can find forgiveness and salvation that will reserve a place for us with God.

But believing is more than simply acknowledging intellectually that Jesus is God. Even the demons who serve Satan -- and Satan himself -- know that. Rather, it is belief so deep that we entrust our lives and our eternity to Christ. We live like we believe it – because we do.

Faith is a strong and powerful thing.
    -- Writer Bill Little on the Horns' belief they could beat OSU

Believe it: Jesus is the way – and the only way
– to eternal life with God.

DAY 98

HERO WORSHIP

Read 1 Samuel 16:1-13.

*"Do not consider his appearance or his height, for . . . the
Lord does not look at the things man looks at. . . . The
Lord looks at the heart" (v. 7).*

Some folks would see Destinee Hooker as a heroine because
she is one of the greatest two-sport athletes in Texas history. Before that, though, her family knew her as one after she slapped
her father hard -- and may have saved his life.

In 2008-09, Hooker was named the Big 12 Conference Female
Athlete of the Year. She was twice a first-team All-America in
volleyball as an outside hitter. Her coach, Jerritt Elliott, called her
"one of the few players in this country that can take over a match
on her own." As a senior in 2009, she led the country in points per
set and drove the Longhorns to the NCAA finals where she had
a career-high 34 kills.

In track and field, she was a four-time NCAA champion and
the NCAA indoor record holder in the high jump. She won six
individual Big 12 titles. In 2006, she helped the Horns win the
NCAA indoor national championship. Thus, Destinee Hooker
has taken her rightful place among the pantheon of brilliant UT
athletes who elicit fans' ongoing adulation.

But back when she was 15, Hooker did something more heroic
than any of her feats as a Longhorn. One evening, she walked into
her parents' bedroom in their home in San Antonio to discover

her mother hysterical and her father passed out on the floor. "Mom ran out of the room to call 911, and dad wasn't moving," Hooker recalled. "My sister ran out of the room crying. I was just like, 'No, this is not happening.'"

So she took control as she would later do so often as a Texas volleyball player. She ran up to her father and started slapping his face. "I hit him hard a few times," Hooker said. Later diagnosed with severe dehydration, her dad finally opened his eyes, looked at his daughter, and smiled.

A hero is commonly thought of as someone who performs brave or dangerous feats that save or protect someone's life – as Destinee Hooker did with her dad. You figure that excludes you.

But ask your son about that when you show him how to bait a hook, or your daughter when you show up for her dance recital. Look into the eyes of those Little Leaguers you help coach or those young people you teach Sunday school to.

Ask God about heroism when you're steady in your faith. For God, a hero is a person with the heart of a servant. And if a hero is a servant who acts to save other's lives, then the greatest hero of all is Jesus Christ.

God seeks heroes today, those who will proclaim the name of their hero – Jesus – proudly and boldly, no matter how others may scoff or ridicule. God knows heroes when he sees them -- by what's in their hearts.

Always good to wake up to the sight of my baby girl.
    -- Ricky Hooker after Destinee slapped him back to consciousness

**God's heroes are those who remain steady
in their faith while serving others.**

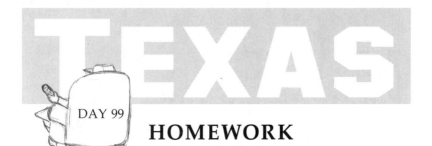

DAY 99

HOMEWORK

Read Joshua 1:1-9.

"Do not let this Book of the Law depart from your mouth; meditate on it day and night, so that you may be careful to do everything written in it. Then you will be prosperous and successful" (v. 8).

Tommy Nobis was more than a little concerned after one of his high-school English teachers advised him not to even bother with applying to the University of Texas. Why not? He couldn't do passing work there, she said.

Nobis is a Longhorn legend. From 1963-65, he averaged nearly twenty tackles a game at linebacker. He was the only sophomore starter for the 1963 11-0 national champions. Nobis was a two-time All-America and three times All-SWC. He also started on offense as a guard; coach Darrell Royal called him "the finest two-way player I have ever seen." As a senior in 1965, he won the Knute Rockne Award for college football's best lineman, the Outland Trophy as the nation's best interior lineman, and the Maxwell Trophy as the country's best college player.

But all that was far in the future when that teacher told young Nobis he wouldn't make it in the classroom. Nobis conceded his teacher had a point: "My grades weren't so good." He seriously considered going to Baylor "because its smaller classes were less intimidating." Finally, though, his desire to play for the Longhorns won out over his worries about the classroom. He told himself that if he didn't give it a try, he would never know.

It wasn't easy. "I've never fooled myself," he once said. "I know I'm not so smart in books. I know my career is football." He came close to flunking out even with the help of Royal's famous "brain coach." (See Devotion No. 36.) "It was a struggle every year, . . . and I just lived with tutors," Nobis recalled.

But he passed in the classroom and excelled on the gridiron.

One of the most enduring illusions of adolescence is that once you graduate from high school and/or college, the homework ends. Life requires constant, ongoing study, however. In many ways, you assemble a life, much as you would a bicycle for your children. You know the drill; even with parts scattered all over the garage, you work undismayed because you can read the instructions and follow them. With the bicycle assembled and ready to race the wind, you nod in satisfaction. Mission completed.

Wouldn't it be great if life, too, had an instruction book, a set of directions that can lead you to a productive, rewarding life so that as its end you can nod in satisfaction and declare "Mission completed"?

It does. Life's instruction book is probably by your bed or on a living room table. It's the Bible, given to you by God to guide you through life. But for it to do you any good, you must read it; you must do your homework.

I was an average student. Football was my priority. That's my biggest regret today.
-- Tommy Nobis

The Bible is God's instruction book
with directions on how to assemble your life.

CLOTHES HORSE

Read Genesis 37:1-11.

*"Israel loved Joseph more than all his children, because
he was the son of his old age: and he made him a coat of
many colours" (v. 3 KJV).*

On the way to a picnic and a baseball game and eager to impress their dates, two students inadvertently set Texas athletes
and their fans on a path to wear orange and white.

In April 1885, Southwestern University invited UT and its new
baseball team to a picnic and a game. The custom then was to
wear colored ribbons to show team loyalty. As the chartered train
was about to leave the Austin station, two UT coeds announced
that no one had any ribbons.

Their dates promptly detrained, sprinted to a general store, and
asked for bolts of fabric. When the shopkeeper asked what colors
they wanted, they replied, "Anything." He sold them two colors
because they were what he had the most of: white, because it was
always in demand for weddings and parties; and orange, because
nobody wanted it and he was stuck with a bunch of it. Thus, UT's
first baseball team was supported by orange and white, but the
University's colors were "christened on a dire and stricken field"
as on a rainy Saturday afternoon, the University lost.

For many seasons, though, uniform colors were subject to the
whims of the individual teams. Early football teams, for instance,
wore gold and white. Those colors were derided as not being

masculine enough, leading the athletic association to resurrect orange and white in 1895. Because the white uniforms were so heard to clean, though, the colors of choice became orange and maroon in 1897. Confusion reigned until the Board of Regents called for an election to settle the matter. By a majority of seven votes, the students, faculty, staff, and alums went with orange and white, harkening back to two guys and their dates in 1885.

Contemporary society proclaims that it's all about the clothes -- or in this case, the uniforms. Buy that new suit or dress, those new shoes, and all the accessories, and you'll be a new person. The changes are only cosmetic, though; under those clothes, you're the same person. Consider Joseph, for instance, prancing about in his pretty new clothes; he was still a spoiled little tattletale whom his brothers detested enough to sell into slavery.

Jesus never taught that we should run around half-naked or wear only second-hand clothes from the local mission. He did warn us, though, against making consumer items such as clothes a priority in our lives.

A follower of Christ seeks to emulate our Lord not through material, superficial means such as wearing special clothing like a robe and sandals. Rather, the disciple desires to match Jesus' inner beauty and serenity -- whether the clothes the Christian wears are the sables of a king or the rags of a pauper.

The bright orange faded, leading other teams to deride the Longhorn football players as 'yellowbellies.'
-- Why coach Clyde Littlefield changed the jerseys to burnt orange

**Where Jesus is concerned, clothes
don't make the person; faith does.**

NOTES
(by Devotion Day Number)

1   when brothers Paul and Ray McLane . . . swelled to about two thousand by kickoff,": John Maher & Kirk Bohls, *Long Live the Longhorns* (New York City: St. Martin's Press, 1993), p. 3.

1   The university team scored on its . . . the 18-16 final look closer than it really was.: Maher & Bohls, p. 4.

1   A lot of guys . . . barbershop quartet they heard.: W.K. Stratton, *Backyard Brawl* (New York City: Three Rivers Press, 2003), p. 74.

2   Darrell Royal was coaching at Mississippi State . . . to have a chance to coach here.: Darrell Royal with John Wheat, *Coach Royal* (Austin: University of Texas Press, 2005), p. 12.

2   "After I got into the coaching profession, I followed closely what was going on: Royal with Wheat, p. 12.

2   He often told Edith how great . . . would do well to talk to him.: Royal with Wheat, p. 17.

2   from interview to hiring took less than five hours.: Royal with Wheat, p. 20.

2   I used to daydream about what it'd be like to coach at Texas.: Royal with Wheat, p. 12.

3   hitting him harder than any opposing team had during the entire CWS.: Cedric Golden, "Six Flags of Texas," *Austin American-Statesman*, June 27, 2005.

3   when he struck out the final batter, . . . Teagarden came running.: Golden, "Six Flags of Texas."

3   Freshman backup catcher Todd Gilfillan . . . the celebration with a broad smile." Cedric Golden, "National Champions 2005 Texas Longhorns," *Austin American-Statesman*, June 28, 2005.

3   Teabag [Taylor Teagarden] really drilled me good.: Golden, "Six Flags of Texas."

4   "I remember all of us just looking at each other and saying, 'This is it,'": Kevin Robbins, "Young Was the Hero," *Austin American-Statesman*, Dec. 31, 2009, http://www.statesman.com/sports/longhorns/young-was-the-hero-but-robisons-stop-helped-157871.html.

4   When the Trojans broke their . . . held on for help to arrive.: Robbins, "Young Was the Hero."

4   I saw it. Read it.: Robbins, "Young Was the Hero."

5   Berry was a junior with . . . by the Russians in 1945.: Bill Little, *Stadium Stories: Texas Longhorns* (Guilford, CN: The Globe Pequot Press, 2005), p. 27.

5   He was 32, married, the father of three children, and had a knee injury.: Little, p. 27.

5   Very few thought [K.L. Berry] would be able . . . [Coach E.J.] Stewart puts his youngsters through.: Maher & Bohls, p. 64.

6   "one of the most revered divers in Texas history.": "Longhorn Hall of Honor: Laura Wilkinson," *TexasSports.com*, Nov. 17, 2009, http://www.texassports.com/genrel/111709aab.html.

6   "I still bleed burnt orange," . . . I just loved being a Longhorn.: "Longhorn Hall of Honor: Laura Wilkinson."

6   "There's nothing like overcoming . . . Nothing feels better.": Amy van Deusen, "Q&A With Olympic Champion Laura Wilkinson," *Women's Health*, http://www.womenshealthmag.com/fitness/laura-wilkinson-interview, Feb. 24, 2011.

6   While she was practicing in March before the 2000 Olympics in Sydney,: "Laura Wilkinson -- 'Do It for Hilary,'" http://sports.jrank.org/pages/5303/Wilkinson-Laura-Do-Hilary.html, Feb. 24, 2011.

6   Wilkinson broke a bone in three . . . goal of reaching the Olympics.: "Longhorn Hall of Honor: Laura Wilkinson."

6   she was in first place . . . and won the gold medal.": "Laura Wilkinson - 'Do It for Hilary.'"

6   When I broke my foot, . . . my vision became very clear again.: "Longhorn Hall of Honor: Laura Wilkinson."

7   "one of the most important women in the history of Texas Longhorns football.: Bill Little, "Bill Little Commentary: Momma's Roses," *TexasSports.com*, Aug. 3, 2009, http://www.texassports.com/sports/m-footbl/spec-rel/080309aab.html, Sept. 10. 2010.

7   Earl Campbell's "high school career . . . school running back in state history." Little, *Stadium Stories*, p. 113.

7   In an age when illegal recruiting offers . . . been bought and sold long enough.": Little, *Stadium Stories*, p. 114.

7   UT assistant coach Ken Dabbs was present . . . so you tell them that.": Little, "Momma's Roses."

7   "she wouldn't have to look at the stars at night through the holes in the roof.": Little, "Momma's Roses."

7   Earl Campbell is the greatest football player . . . is the best coach there ever was.: Emily Nasits, "Earl Campbell: The College Years," *Echoes of Texas Football: The Greatest Stories Ever Told*, ed. Ken Samelson (Chicago: Triumph Books, 2006), p. 65.

8   "It was high drama at Cowboys Stadium,": Suzanne Halliburton, "Ain't That a Kick," *Austin American-Statesman*, Dec. 6, 2009, p. C01.

8   a "brief, scary moment,": Bill Little, "Bill Little Commentary: Wait Just a Second," *TexasSports.com*, Dec. 18, 2009, http://www.texassports.com/sports/m-footbl/spec-rel/121809aaa.html.

8   McCoy was sure he hadn't, . . . signaled that the game was over.: Halliburton, "Ain't That a Kick."

8   The review, said the conference's . . . quoted Jeremiah 17:7 to his kicker: Halliburton, "Ain't That a Kick."

8   I think in Lincoln, it'll be the clock. And in Austin, it'll be the comeback.: Halliburton, "Ain't That a Kick."

9   "We were supposed to win . . . "It [was] all set up for us.": Greg Garber, "Seniors, Anger, Fuel First Perfect Season," *ESPN.com*, Feb. 28, 2009, http://sports.espn.go.com/ncw/news/story?page=garber_perfect_texas, Sept. 27, 2010.

9   "It made us mad." Garber.

9   "a purely selfish matter . . . unwelcome misfortune or frustration.": Bruce T. Dahlberg, "Anger," *The Interpreter's Dictionary of the Bible* (Nashville: Abingdon Press, 1962), Vol. 1, p. 136.

10   Layne threw an ill-advised interception . . . of all things -- a Layne interception.: Bill Little, "Bill Little
      Commentary: The Quarterback's Tale," *TexasSports.com*, Nov. 1, 2007, http://www.texassports.com/
      sports/m-footbl/spec-rel/110107aad.html.
11   In the spring of 2001, he . . . and gave it to Archer.: Bill Little, "Bill Little Commentary: A Touch of Class,"
      TexasSports.com, Dec. 17, 2001, http://www.texassports.com/sports/m-footbl/spec-rel/121701aaa.html.
12   she wasn't recruited by the Longhorns out of high school.: Mark Swanson, "Final Four Is Better Late Than
      Never for UT's Dickson," *Austin American-Statesman*, Dec. 16, 2010, p. C01.
12   she had played three years for UVa . . . "She's a great story,": Swanson, "Final Four Is Better Late Than
      Never."
13   "My dream was taken from me," . . . "I'd have to say no.": Kevin Robbins, "At the End of Journey Never
      Begun, Peace," *Austin American-Statesman*, Nov. 25, 2010, p. A01.
14   In the game's first 40 minutes, . . . leading rusher with 54 yards and a score.: "College Football: Duke's Day,"
      Time, Jan. 10, 1964, http://www.time.cnn.com/time/magazine/article/0.9171,875532-1,000.html, Sept.
      24, 2010.
14   During the game, he found a 50-cent . . . out of the mass of humanity.: Richardson, p. 109.
14   Carlisle reached into his pants . . . "because that doesn't look real good.": Richardson, p. 110.
15   "I was the guy who was carefree . . . didn't know the value of academics.": "Terrence Rencher: Completing
      a Journey," *TexasSports.com*, Dec. 8, 2007, http://www.texassports.com/sports/m-baskbl/spec-rel/
      120807aaa.html, Sept. 27, 2010.
15   As a sophomore, he was suspended for two games because of academic problems.: Mark Rosner, "A Study
      in Persistence," *Austin American-Statesman*, Dec. 12, 2007, p. C01.
15   When he finished his pro career, . . . He called it "a great day.": "Terrence Rencher: Completing a Journey."
15   I always knew that I was going to get my degree.: "Terrence Rencher: Completing a Journey."
16   When Longhorn football coaches first saw . . . to bulk up his 6-foot-2 frame,: Suzanne Halliburton,
      "Scrawny Kid, Hefty Hopes," *Austin American-Statesman*, Nov. 11, 1991, p. D1.
16   His first job was joining the other . . . speed and good hands,": Halliburton, "Scrawny Kid, Hefty Hopes."
17   The season included the introduction . . . showed the cheerleader his creation.: Maher and Bohls, p. 131.
17   Clark tried the Hook-'em,-Horns sign on . . . the object of such great interest.": Maher and Bohls, p. 132.
17   Ours has far surpassed A&M's sign.: Maher and Bohls, p. 132.
18   Nobody thought too much about a 59-52 loss the Texas women suffered to Texas A&M: Richard Pennington,
      Longhorn Hoops: The History of Texas Basketball (Austin: University of Texas Press, 1998), p. 288.
18   Her starters were Retha Swindell, . . . brand new Special Events Center.: Pennington, p. 286.
18   In January of that season, the Texas women had their first-ever game programs.: Pennington, p. 288.
18   It would be the next season before they would have their first media guide.: Pennington, p. 289.
18   The people at the University of Texas . . . the women whatever it takes to be the best.: Pennington, p. 284.
19   "the most versatile player I've had in 34 years.": Kirk Bohls, "His Strong Faith Carries Hall in Football, Life,"
      Austin American-Statesman, Oct. 28, 2007, p. C01.
19   for Hall, BMOC meant "Big Man . . . 'God bless Chris Hall.": Bohls, "His Strong Faith Carries Hall."
20   "probably the most dominant athlete ever to play a sport for Texas.": Peter Bean, "Catching Up with Cat
      Osterman," *Burnt Orange Nation*, Jan. 3, 2011, http://www.burntorangenation.com/2011/1/3/1911256/
      catching-up-with-cat-osterman.
20   she struck out the first nine batters . . . But it all worked out.": Olin Buchanan, "She's Purrfect," *The Austin
      American-Statesman*, May 22, 2005.
20   I wasn't going to be the one to ruin it.: Buchanan, "She's Purrfect."
21   When the 8-year-old Brewer met Texas . . . a "pretty average" quarterback in high school.: Maher and Bohls,
      p. 205.
21   He nevertheless confidently told Texas . . . you will get a chance.": Richardson, *Tales from the Texas Longhorns*
      (Champaign, IL: Sports Publishing L.L.C., 2003) p. 149.
21   Receiver Herkie Walls told Brwer, "You are not the No. 2 quarterback any more, so don't play like it.":
      Richardson, p. 149.
22   Harrison Stafford showed up in Austin and announced he wanted to play football.: Bill Little, "Bill Little
      Commentary: Harrison Stafford Dies, Second Horn Hall of Famer Passes," *TexasSports.com*, Dec. 2,
      2004, http://www.texassports.com/sports/m-footbl/spec-rel/120204aaa.html.
22   His first Texas uniform was . . . and hurt a couple of men.: Maher and Bohls, p. 75.
22   who refused to play with a helmet because he couldn't see when he wore it.: Maher and Bohls, p. 71.
22   At Stafford's first practice, he flattened . . . hardest I've ever been hit.": Maher and Bohls, p. 75.
22   Stafford was a star hurdler . . . the long jump, the shot put, and the javelin.: Maher and Bohls, p. 75.
22   "I don't remember anything of the game," . . . back for a week or more.: Maher and Bohls, p. 76.
22   I had to put a schedule of my classes . . . where I was supposed to be.: Maher and Bohls, pp. 76-77.
23   Man, I can have some fun with this.": Bill Little, "Bill Little Commentary: While You Were Sleeping," *Texas
      Sports.com*, Sept. 7, 2008, http://www.texassports.com/sports/m-footbl/spec-rel/090708aah.html.
23   Defensive backs coach Duane Akina . . . when he realized he could have some fun.: Little, "While You Were
      Sleeping."
24   The rules then called for the teams to draw . . . "Yeah, I'm sure,": Wilbur Evans and Bill Little, *Texas
      Longhorn Baseball: Kings of the Diamond* (Huntsville, AL: The Strode Publishers,
      1983), p. 351.
24   When the game ended, Gustafson . . . we've got one more to go.": Evans and Little, p. 352.

24   who only months before had . . . wondered if he would ever walk again,: Evans and Little, p. 354.
25   The play was called Steelers Roll Left. . . . people called me crazy,": Tim Layden, "Underdogs to the
       Cornhuskers," *Sports Illustrated Presents Texas Longhorns Football* (New York City: Time Inc. Home
       Entertainment, 2009), p. 39.
25   "Calling that play took guts,": Layden, p. 39.
25   If you are going to be a champion, you have to go for it.: Richardson, p. 173.
26   One of the primary reasons for . . . a higher profile in basketball.: Bill Little, *Hoop Tales: Texas Longhorns
       Men's Basketball* (Guilford, CN: The Globe Pequot Press, 2008), p. 128.
26   "Recruits were leaving Texas and starring at . . . into the hearts of the [Texas] fans.": Little, *Hoop Tales*, p. 128.
26   With "his contagious smile and . . . a great ambassador for the school.: Little, *Hoop Tales*, p. 135.
26   "He made it all right to come to Texas,": Little, *Hoop Tales*, p. 136.
26   [T.J. Ford has] done more for Texas basketball . . . He changed the attitude of Texas basketball.: Little, *Hoop
       Tales*, p. 136.
27   "Texas has to develop a football . . . "that bloodletting up at Dallas.": Bill Little, "Bill Little Commentary:
       When The Shouting Has Gone," *TexasSports.com*, Oct. 10, 2008, http://www.texassports.com/sports/
       m-footbl/spec-rel/101008aab.html.
27   As a dyed-in-the-wool purist, Royal opposed the change.: Little, "When the Shouting Has Gone."
27   Royal had decided on Friday . . . only the ear flaps were showing,": Little, "When the Shouting Has Gone."
27   We were shooting for the win.: Little, "When the Shouting Has Gone."
28   The flu that ravaged the world in 1918 . . . including the Texas-Oklahoma game.: John Maher, "In 1918, UT's
       Football Foes Included War, Flu Pandemic," *Austin American-Statesman*, May 3, 2009, p. A01.
28   "war planners were turning college . . . and waited to be drafted.: Maher, "In 1918, UT's Football Foes."
28   closed to the public: Maher, "In 1918, UT's Football Foes."
28   guard Joe Spence fill ill after the A&M game and died.: Maher, "In 1918, UT's Football Foes."
28   All semblance of regular college life was gone.: Maher, "In 1918, UT's Football Foes."
29   In 1949, a Texas student named . . . land in a pretty girl's lap.": Mark Rosner, "Gregory Has Been Good to
       Howdens," *Austin American-Statesman*, Sept. 1, 2004.
29   Debi saw Lynn shooting in . . . was "kind of flirtatious.": Rosner, "Gregory Has Been Good to Howdens."
29   Lynn constantly reminded his . . . into a men's rest room.: Rosner, "Gregory Has Been Good to Howdens."
29   I love Gregory Gym. I still get a thrill going there.: Rosner, "Gregory Has Been Good to Howdens."
30   "and a 30-game winning streak that rocked the college world": Richardson, p. 61.
30   Royal wanted to find a way . . . "piddled around in his yard with his son": Maher and Bohls, p. 164.
30   Quarterback Eddie Phillips recalled that . . . using salt and paper shakers.: Richardson, p. 62.
30   "We all had a lot of doubts," . . . because it eliminated my position,": Maher and Bohls, p. 165.
30   The sellout crowd booed lustily. "I can't say I disagreed with them,": Maher and Bohls, p. 165.
30   the Longhorns broke six conference team offense records that season: Richardson, p. 65.
30   It's kind of scary when you're told you're not going to block some guy [the defensive end].: Maher and
       Bohls, p. 165.
31   their "suffocating defense and pressure-resistant kicker.": Maher and Bohls, p. 207.
31   "I knew I would be an average . . . good field goal kicker if that's all I did.": Richardson, p. 151.
31   "No one thought we could win,": Maher and Bohls, p. 214.
31   "Fred was saying we need the field . . . endorsed the kick, Akers relented.: Maher and Bohls, p. 214.
31   Of the 32 wins Ward was involved in, his field goals made the difference in 13 of them.: Maher and Bohls,
       p. 215.
32   UT's first women's intercollegiate basketball game . . . an intramural, interclass affair.": Pennington, p. 270.
32   this "visionary in directing physical education" "was among the most prominent women on campus.":
       Pennington, p. 270.
32   She was also, however, dead set against . . . by money and skewed educational values.": Pennington, p. 270.
32   She totally disapproved of pampered, elite . . . "too physically and emotionally strenuous for women.":
       Pennington, p. 271.
32   they were all undersized to discourage basketball competition.: Pennington, p. 272.
33   "Things had been down . . . "There was a loser mentality.": Little, *Stadium Stories*, p. 41.
33   As disheartened Texas fans streamed toward the exits,: Little, *Stadium Stories*, p. 41.
33   Bible instructed the band director to play . . . stand and listen to the song.: Maher and Bohls, p. 98.
33   quarterback Johnny Gill made up a play in the huddle.: Little, *Stadium Stories*, p. 41.
33   Ecstatic Longhorn fans stormed the field; . . . to clear it for the extra point.: Little, *Stadium Stories*, p. 42.
33   "That play and that victory changed our outlook,": Little, *Stadium Stories*, p. 42.
33   "before that, everything was down. After that, everything was on the way up.": Little, *Stadium Stories*, p. 42.
33   It was the renaissance of Texas football.: Little, *Stadium Stories*, p. 42.
34   making seven of its first ten . . . with 5:18 gone in the game.: Wendell Barnhouse, "Streak Busters,"
       Big12Sports.com, Jan. 22, 2011, http://www.big12sports.com/ViewArticle.
34   They went into the KU game . . . "We took that away from them.": Barnhouse.
34   Time to start another streak.: Barnhouse.
35   his locker with his No. 44 jersey . . . mementos of Pittman's brief time as a Longhorn.: Bill Little, *Texas
       Football: Yesterday & Today* (Lincolnwood, IL: West Side Publishing, 2009), p. 117.
35   Brett Robin scored with 36 . . . total at 44 in Pittman's honor.: Little, *Texas Football*, p. 117.
36   discovered to his dismay that fifteen of his would-be players were academically ineligible.: Roy Terrell,

"Kickoff in Dixie," *Sports Illustrated*, Sept. 29, 1958, http://sportsillustrated.cnn.com/vault/article/magazine/MAG1002884/index.htm, June 13, 2010.

36   "We had enough players," . . . we much as we [needed] an academic counselor.": Maher and Bohls, p. 137.

36   I guess you would have to say . . . football players were academically ineligible.: Terrell.

36   "It was the best move I ever made,": Maher and Bohls, p. 137.

36   [Having academic counseling] is like religion. Everyone should have some of it.: Terrell.

37   described by one writer as "dismal.": Mike Finger, "Comeback Hooked for UT in Alamo Bowl," *San Antonio Express-News*, Dec. 29, 2012, http://www.mysanantonio.com/sports/alamo_bowl/article/Comeback.

37   At halftime, Brown told . . .they had planned on doing.: Finger, "Comeback Hooked for UT."

37   Hey, forget it. Let's go.: Finger, "Comeback Hooked for UT."

38   would get his kicks by clearing out the riffraff in waterfront bars.: Maher and Bohls, p. 119.

38   "They beat us like a drum," . . . broke all their legs and never walked again.": Maher and Bohls, p. 119.

39   To test out the new plumbing, . . . a massive simultaneous flush.: Little, *Stadium Stories*, p. 32.

39   didn't like the rule banning . . . "Shoot, he almost made it.": Little, *Hoop Tales*, pp. 91-92.

39   As a memento of the legendary win, . . . and was killed at Iwo Jima.: Little, *Stadium Stories*, p. 28.

39   At the Japanese surrender ceremony . . . it was Chevigny's pen.: Little, *Stadium Stories*, p. 30.

40   "one of the most unique and charismatic . . . from left-center to right center field.: "Before There was a Longhorn, There were . . . Dogs, Pigs, and Billy Goats?: Clark's Billy Goat Hill," *Burnt Orange Living*, March 22, 2010, http://burntorangeliving.wordpress.com/tag/texas-baseball.

40   The cliff received its name . . . a goat path in left-center.: "Clark's Billy Goat Hill."

40   Clarence Pfeil and Pete Layden, teammates . . . at using Billy Goat Hill to their advantage.: Evans and Little, p. 411.

40   Some Texas center fielders adopted . . . to help cover the full outfield.: "Clark's Billy Goat Hill."

40   One adventuresome A&M center fielder . . . via the safe goat path.: Evans and Little, p. 411.

41   The quarterback's fellow seniors joined him in a celebratory dogpile: Suzanne Halliburton, "An Emphatic 43rd," *Austin American-Statesman*, Nov. 22, 2009, p. C01.

41   "I don't think he could have scripted it any better,": Halliburton, "An Emphatic 43rd."

41   McCoy and the crowd didn't want . . . a few high-fives along the way.": Halliburton, "An Emphatic 43rd."

41   What is important to me is winning.: Halliburton, "An Emphatic 43rd."

42   the coaches spotted something they . . . sometimes didn't secure the football.: Bill Little, "Bill Little Commentary, "The Learning Curve," *TexasSports.com*, Sept. 13, 2004, http://www.texassports.com/sports/m-footbl/spec-rel/091304aab.html.

42   It was textbook training, exactly as he had been coached.: Little, "The Learning Curve."

43   in an effort to give his program some national exposure: Little, *Hoop Tales*, p. 18.

43   coaches and players alike were expected . . . "But it's stopped going up.": Little, *Hoop Tales*, pp. 23, 25.

43   Gray gave Samsing a new assignment . . . with your finger in my belt, and don't let me get up.": Little, *Hoop Tales*, p. 27.

43   (and friend of Jack Gray): Little, *Hoop Tales*, p. 27.

44   The media crucified Royal, criticizing . . . out of touch with the contemporary player.: Nasits, p. 63.

44   In the locker room after the season-ending . . . described Campbell as "a loyal, caring friend.": Nasits, p. 63.

44   When Earl Campbell takes someone as a friend, there's nothing he wouldn't do for them.: Nasits, p. 63.

45   "would alter the course of Texas football history.": "Tom Campbell Profile," *TexasSports.com*, http://www.texassports.com/genrel/campbell_tom00.html.

45   "We were walk-ons." . . . so the real players could practice.": Suzanne Halliburton, "Campbell's Memories of Irish at Fore This Week," *Austin American-Statesman*, Sept. 18, 1995, p. D1.

46   a play Texas had not run since 1980.: Pat Putnam, "A Little Texas Ingenuity," *Sports Illustrated Presents Texas Longhorns Football* (New York City: Time Inc. Home Entertainment, 2009), p. 35.

46   Play 24 was a simple, quick . . . and went behind that block: Putnam, p. 35.

47   The new team in town held its first practice . . . that will go down in history.": Mark Wangrin, "Texas' Softball Dream Will Get Real Today," *The Austin American-Statesman*, Feb. 15, 1996, p. D2.

48   He was with his offensive mates . . . we'll take it play by play.": Austin Murphy, "With a Stunning Comeback Victory," *Sports Illustrated Presents Texas Longhorns Football* (New York City: Time Inc. Home Entertainment, 2009), p. 41.

48   who made a leaping backward catch in double coverage: Joe Funk and Rob Doster, eds., *Texas Pride* (Chicago: Triumph Books, 2006), p. 32.

48   All the kids that watched TV said nobody gave us any chance and you can't win here.: Funk, p. 32.

49   "Bill was one of the best athletes . . . cartilage damage in his knee: Maher and Bohls, p. 160.

49   required surgery at year's end. . . . my body I was so taped up.: Maher and Bohls, p. 163.

49   In the second game, Royal benched him . . . "You can't do any worse.": Maher and Bohls, p. 165.

49   When Royal told Bradley he was . . . I decided I was going to become a leader.": Maher and Bohls, p. 166.

49   against Rice, he flattened a defender . . . a defensive back out of Bradley.: Maher and Bohls, p. 167.

49   "ambivalent, vacillating, impulsive, unsubmissive." John MacArthur, *Twelve Ordinary Men* (Nashville: W Publishing Group, 2002), p. 39.

49   "the greatest preacher among . . . "dominant figure" in the church's birth.: MacArthur, p. 39.

49   I was still a captain and I'd show 'em what I have made of.: Maher and Bohls, p. 166.

50   As Lancaster's senior season wound down . . . try out for the basketball team.: Natalie England, "Texas Student-Athlete Spotlight: Sarah Lancaster," *Big12Sports.com*,

Jan. 6, 2011, http://www.big12sports.com/ViewArticle.dbml?DB_OEM_ID=10410&ATCLID=205072.

50   The senior treated the idea like the joke she thought it was.: England, "Texas Student-Athlete Spotlight."

50   She had given up basketball . . . approached her about joining the team.: Rick Cantu, "Game, Set, Match, Switch: UT Player Swaps out Nets," *Austin American-Statesman*, Feb. 5, 2011, p. C01.

50   recording the fastest time in the mile . . . nineteen seasons of college coaching.: Cantu, "Game, Set, Match, Switch."

50   "She's a winner,": England, "Texas Student-Athlete Spotlight."

50   All the tennis girls thought it was the coolest thing ever.: Cantu, "Game, Set, Match, Switch."

51   Part of his preparation for the game . . . concerns about his pass defense.: Mark Wangrin, "Horns Pick and Bruise," *Austin American-Statesman*, Sept. 6, 1997, p. C1.

51   That was something I never could have imagined.: Wangrin, "Horns Pick and Bruise."

52   for the first time in school history. . . . injuries suffered against SMU.: Jim Nicar, "The Rose Bowl That Was (Almost) in Austin," Dec. 21, 2009, http://www.utexas.edu/know/2009/12/21/rose_bowl_almost/.

52   some students consulted Madam . . . to hex the Aggies.: Nicar, "The Rose Bowl."

52   "They needed something to show the team they were behind them,": Little, *Stadium Stories*, p. 45.

52   Red candles showed up everywhere . . . a uniting of the football team and its fans.: Nicar, "The Rose Bowl."

52   We broke that jinx over there.: Maher and Bohls, p. 104.

53   The Tennessee athletic department cooked up . . . that even I have for promoting the game.": Hank Hersch, "A Texas Waltz in Tennessee," *Sports Illustrated*, Dec. 21, 1987, http://sportsillustrated.cnn.com/vault/article/magazine/MAG1066871/index.htm.

54   They threw $4 million cash at him . . . scrubbed tile for spending money: Kirk Bohls, "Good Fella," *Echoes of Texas Football: The Greatest Stories Ever Told*, ed. Ken Samelson (Chicago: Triumph Books, 2006), p. 69.

54   speculation grew that head coach John . . . for the NFL if that happened.: "Ricky Williams: What It Means to Be a Longhorn," *TexasSports.com*, June 26, 2008, http://www.texassports.com/sports/m-footbl/spec-rel/062608aaa.html.

54   a player who had worked on Sunday mornings . . . and earned $4.95 for his effort.: Bohls, p. 69.

54   felt that if had been healthy, . . . want to end my career on a game like that,": "Ricky Williams: What It Means to Be a Longhorn."

54   They had a long conversation . . . do whatever it is that you really want to do.': Little, *Stadium Stories*, p. 122.

55   In a game against SMU, a press box spotter . . . it had been six.: Bill Little, "Bill Little Commentary: Honoring a Champion," *TexasSports.com*, May 7, 2002, http://www.texassports.com/sports/m-footbl/spec-rel/050702aab.html.

55   The problem was on the sideline, . . . following Sisemore into the end zone.: Little, "Honoring a Champion."

55   In his white uniform and the . . . against the gray November sky.: Little, "Honoring a Champion."

56   Texas trailed 3-2 with two outs . . . saw the ball roll away.": Evans and Little, p. 321.

56   But not one of the umps . . . a rule interpretation, the call stood.: Evans and Little, p. 322.

56   Texas was right -- dead right . . . as if it had been dead wrong.: Evans and Little, p. 322.

57   He wrote to other large . . . objections to A&M head football coach Charley Moran.: Maher and Bohls, p. 41.

57   In 1908, fans and students got into . . . stab wounds to his head in the scuffle.: Maher and Bohls, pp. 28-29.

57   Before the 1911 game, officials from both . . . two schools were completely severed.: Maher and Bohls, p. 35.

57   Only when A&M announced that Moran would not be back for the 1915 season was the new league formed.: Maher and Bohls, p. 41.

57   A&M has stretched forth the olive . . . opportunity to renew amicable relations.: Maher and Bohols, p. 42.

58   the season before had watched . . . as a spotter for the radio broadcasters.: Maher and Bohls, p. 195.

58   "untested reserve with little playing experience": Little, *Stadium Stories*, p. 123.

58   McEachern's teammates carried him off the field.: Richardson, p. 93.

58   Randy [McEachern] came in and took it . . . showed everybody how good he was.: Maher and Bohls, p. 195.

58   who became a folk hero in one afternoon: "Randy McEachern: Profile," *TexasSports.com*, http://www.texassports.com/genrel/mceachern_randy00.html.

59   "Chev, you're doing a fine . . . to be the head coach.": Gene Schoor, *100 Years of Texas Longhorn Football* (Dallas: Taylor Publishing Company, 1993), p. 1.

59   Notre Dame athletic officials decided he was too young for the job.: Bobby Hawthorne, *Longhorn Football: An Illustrated History* (Austin: University of Texas Press, 2007), p. 23.

59   "he was bitterly heartbroken.": Schoor, p. 2.

59   Chevigny invoked Rockne, his dead mother, . . . kickoff, the Texas players were frothing.": Hawthorne, p. 23.

59   "signaled the arrival of the Southwest Conference as a major player on the national scene.": Hawthorne, p. 23.

59   We did it. We won. [We] beat Notre Dame. A dream come true.: Schoor, p. 4.

60   "What I really wanted was a good . . . didn't see how I could make it.": Little, *Hoop Tales*, p. 72.

60   had been hired in 1967 to return . . . antiquated Gregory Gym, which seated only 7,800.: Little, *Hoop Tales*, pp. 74-75.

60   seeing himself "as an ordinary man seeking an education": Little, *Hoop Tales*, p. 72.

60   he had broken all but one of Texas' scoring and rebounding records.: Little, *Hoop Tales*, p. 81.

60   for the highest sum ever paid to a basketball player: Little, *Hoop Tales*, p. 82.

62   whom coach Bibb Falk had put in "to give him a chance to letter,": Evans and Little, p. 281.

62   "When the ball was hit, . . . ever was or ever will be, rose as one.": Evans and Little, p. 283.

62   Now how's that for a comeback?: Evans and Little, p. 283.

206

63   On the bus ride to the stadium, Royal . . . but he noted what his coach said.: Little, *Stadium Stories*, p. 103.

63   "perhaps the most significant play in Texas history": Little, *Stadium Stories*, p. 106.

64   let their hair grow long to protect their heads in the absence of helmets.: Little, *Stadium Stories*, p. 5.

64   When the game ended, John Henry . . . "It's nowhere near sundown.": Little, *Stadium Stories*, p. 10.

64   "The professional game of foot ball . . . a lot of running thrown in.": Little, *Stadium Stories*, p. 5.

64   "We were getting pretty swell-headed by the time Missouri came along,": Little, *Stadium Stories*, p. 16.

64   They "came long and tore up our . . . quit both school and football permanently.: Little, *Stadium Stories*, p. 16.

64   I sneaked out of town that night and cut out my 'football course' at The University of Texas.: Little, *Stadium Stories*, p. 16.

65   Nash "looked like she had gone a couple . . . who was 7 at the time.": Rick Cantu, "Kathleen Nash Known for Toughness in UT Career That's About to End," *The Austin American-Statesman*, March 1, 2011.

65   "one of the most distinguished basketball players in University of Texas history.": Cantu, "Kathleen Nash Known for Toughness."

66   We've got them right where we want them,": Maher and Bohls, p. 147.

66   exasperated Treadwell no end because . . . right where it wanted them.: Maher and Bohls, pp. 147-48.

66   On third down, Arkansas 218-lb. . . . one of the most famous of all Longhorn photographs.: Maher and Bohls, p. 148.

66   [Johnny Treadwell and Pat Culpepper] just loved . . . you had to run right at them.: Maher and Bohls, p. 147.

67   Imperturbable as always,: Asher Price, "Texas Longhorns: National Champions, Party!" *Austin American-Statesman*, Jan. 16, 2006.

67   The cheerleaders, the band, Bevo, . . . players wore jeans not pads,": Price, "Texas Longhorns."

67   the partygoers started lining up . . . mad I'm not still on the team,": Price, "Texas Longhorns."

67   They jumped to their feet . . . showed up amid swirling smoke.: Price, "Texas Longhorns."

67   This is one night when we can . . . because we're number one.": Price, "Texas Longhorns."

68   He knocked SMU's best back out of the game . . . "stuffed the cake between the crevices of my teeth.": Maher and Bohls, p. 109.

68   Darrell Royal told me once I hit him harder than anyone.: Maher and Bohls, p. 115.

69   "This team is a family," . . . you need to come together as a team.": "National Championship Moments: 1995 Women's Tennis," *TexasSports.com*, http://www.texassports.com/sports/w-tennis/spec-rel/120406aaa.html.

69   On the eve of the NCAA Tournament quarterfinals, . . . and volunteer assistant Lea Sauls.: John Maher, "Handling Life's Overhead Smashes," *Austin American-Statesman*, May 23, 1993, p. C1.

69   I knew it was hard because . . . families are more important.: Maher, "Handling Life's Overhead Smashes."

70   When World War I broke out, he was forgotten and left on the farm.: Richardson, p. 7.

70   he was the main course at a homecoming the 1920 team.: Richardson, p. 8.

70   Theo Bellmont, UT's first athletic . . . died a few days later.: "Before There was a Longhorn, There Were . . . Dogs, Pigs, and Billy Goats?: A Dog Named Pig," *Burnt Orange Living*, March 22, 2010, http://burntorangeliving.wordpress.com/tag/texas-baseball, Feb. 25, 2011.

70   He lay in state in the front of the Co-op in a casket draped with orange and white ribbon.: Richardson, p. 9.

70   Hundreds turned out to pay . . . near the old law building.: "A Dog Named Pig."

70   The University went without a mascot . . . a fixture at UT football games until 1966.: Richardson, p. 8.

70   Pig's Dead -- Dog Gone: Richardson, p. 9.

71   Somehow, you had to believe they had one last miracle left in them.": Bill Little, "Bill Little Commentary: A Rose-Colored Miracle," *TexasSports.com*, Jan. 2, 2005, http://www.texassports.com/sports/m-footbl/spec-rel/010205aaa.html.

71   ABC announcer Keith Jackson asked, "How in the world?" as Young crossed the goal line.: Tim Layden, "Vince Young Will Not Let Up," *Sports Illustrated Presents Texas Longhorns Football* (New York City: Time Inc. Home Entertainment, 2009), p. 64.

72   Namath tried a quarterback sneak. . . . cold just short of the goal line.: Little, *Stadium Stories*, p. 89.

73   The selection of UT's most golden moments . . . the Cougars' dominance of the Southwest Conference.: "Top 100 Moments in Texas Men's Basketball History," *TexasSports.com*, http://www.texassports.com/sports/m-baskbl/spec-rel/top-100-moments.html.

74   Memorial Day weekend in 2006, . . . supper they had left waiting and ready.: Bill Little, "Bill Little Commentary: Colt McCoy -- Memorial Day Rescue," *TexasFootball.com*, June 8, 2006, http://www.mackbrown-texasfootball.com/sports/m-footbl/spec-rel/060806aaa.html.

74   That's that Texas quarterback. I'm an Aggie, but I'm proud of that kid.: Little, "Colt McCoy -- Memorial Day Rescue."

75   In 1902, UT student and musician Lewis Johnson . . . had a song that even today it calls its own.: Jim Nicar, "The Origins of 'The Eyes of Texas,'" *Longhorn Band/University of Texas at Austin: History of School and Fight Songs*, http://mbe187.music.utexas.edu/Longhornband/History/Songs.aspx, Sept. 13, 2010.

76   The Horns were four-touchdown underdogs: Maher and Bohls, p. 99.

76   "I was scared to death . . . athlete's mind into thinking positive,": Maher and Bohls, p. 99.

76   Doss then told Crain he could get behind A&M's defensive backs.: Maher and Bohls, p. 99.

76   "the most famous reception in Longhorn history for almost three decades.: Maher and Bohls, p. 98.

76   "a twisting, over-the-head catch: Little, *Texas Football: Yesterday & Today*, p. 29.

76   "a crushing 7-0 defeat [on] perhaps the greatest team in Aggie history: Little, *Texas Football*, p. 29.

76 just what end Wally Scott claimed . . . made the catch with his eyes closed.: Maher and Bohls, p. 98.

76 Look at the picture in the T Room . . . I can promise you [Doss'] eyes were shut.: Maher and Bohols, p. 98.

77 The Irish coaches figured they . . . went down and got it: Dan Jenkins, "A Gamble in the Closing Moments Gave Texas a Cotton Bowl Win over Notre Dame and Another National Title," *Sports Illustrated Presents Texas Longhorns Football* (New York City: Time Inc. Home Entertainment, 2009), p. 33.

77 When you're Number 1, you've got to try to stay that way or get carried out feet first.: Jenkins, p. 33.

78 Darrell Royal and his coaches . . .asked him how he knew about it.: Richardson, p. 63.

78 The sister of one of the Houston players . . . Yeoman had invented in 1964.: Richardson, p. 63.

78 a Houston sportswriter came up with . . . offered the name "wishbone.": Little, *Stadium Stories*, p. 100.

78 In the Wishbone, all you had to do was be a little afraid.: Richardson, p. 64.

79 "In my 41 years of coaching, . . . best pitching performance I've ever seen.": Cedric Golden, "It Was So Long," *Austin American-Statesman*, June 1, 2009, p. A01.

79 This was truly a once-in-a-lifetime experience.: Golden, "It Was So Long."

80 Sportswriters openly called Blair . . . They ridiculed the Orange Bowl: Maher and Bohls, p. 120.

80 "About seven or eight of us seniors were married," . . .the players agreed to play the game.: Maher and Bohls, p. 120.

80 He predicted Georgia would set an Orange Bowl scoring record.: Maher and Bohls, p. 120.

80 "They scored the most points for a losing team in Orange Bowl history,": Maher and Bohls, p. 120.

80 The next time you writers call a team third-rate, you're going to have to play them yourselves.: Maher and Bohls, p. 120.

81 For some forty years, female athletes . . . without any extra compensation of course.: Pennington, p. 274.

81 In October 1966, she held tryouts . . . owned by a player or borrowed from somebody's friend.: Pennington, p. 275.

81 The players were just in a daze. . . . and they wouldn't hear it.: Pennington, p. 277.

82 "We didn't get much respect from the media on both sides of the ball,": Tom Dienhart, "Leapin' Longhorns," *Echoes of Texas Football*, Ken Samelson, ed. (Chicago: Triumph Books, 2006), p. 41.

82 "heard anyone with a microphone . . . teams in college football history.": Dienhart, p. 40.

82 "When the clock struck midnight, the burnt-orange challengers would turn back into pumpkins.": Dienhart, p. 40.

82 "We don't have to be the greatest . . . greatest team (in the title game).": Funk and Doster, eds., *Texas Pride*, p. 12.

82 Mack Brown told USC quarterback Matt Leinart was "a classic game.": Dienhart, p. 40.

82 If you have to hand it over . . . that's a heck of a team to do that for.: Funk and Doster, eds., *Texas Pride*, p. 12.

83 "I don't know how I got by," . . . Gregory Gym each day for 50 cents an hour.": Bill Little, "Bill Little Commentary: Hugh Wolfe -- The First of Many," *TexasSports.com*, April 26, 2007, http://www.texassports.com/sports/m-footbl/spec-rel/042607aab.html.

83 He signed the contact without . . . "a lot of money, then.": Little, "Hugh Wolfe -- The First of Many."

84 Rick Barnes realized what kind of . . . the off-season was their time, not his.: Randy Riggs, "Barnes' Hungry Horns Hold Court in All Seasons," *Austin American-Statesman*, June 18, 2000, p. C1.

84 That first day on the job, . . . last-place teams in our league.": Riggs, "Barnes' Hungry Horns."

84 If you want to be good, . . . You've got to get out and go.: Riggs, "Barnes' Hungry Horns."

85 Texas' "maiden voyage into the Big 12" . . . and a new name for the stadium.: Mark Wangrin, "It Pours, and Texas Reigns," *Austin American-Statesman*, Sept. 1, 1996, p. C1.

85 "a thunderstorm that would have sent . . . and lofted a 10-yard punt.": Wangrin, "It Pours, and Texas Reigns."

85 The refs decided the lightning was . . . amounted to a "Royal flush.": Wangrin, "It Pours, and Texas Reigns."

85 The wind started howling. Then we looked behind us and saw lightning.: Mary Ann Roser and Mark Rosner, "UT 40 -- Missouri 10: Big 12's Stormy Start," *Austin American-Statesman*, Sept. 1, 1996, p. A1.

86 "There just weren't that many high school . . . didn't even know what the sport was": Pamela LeBlanc, "Launching a New Sport," *Austin American-Statesman*, May 1, 2002.

86 I'm making something of my life. . . . be able to do anything like that.: LeBlanc, "Launching a New Sport."

87 Mack Brown started the tradition in 1998:: Little, *Stadium Stories*, p. 108.

87 Steinmark had played for some time . . . the Monday after the Arkansas win,: Maher and Bohls, p. 176.

87 President Richard Nixon phoned after the . . . the game ball in the dressing room.: Maher and Bohls, p. 176.

87 Mother, if God wants my leg, we'll have to give it to Him.: Maher & Bohls, p. 176.

88 "Texas's answer to Jim Thorpe and Bo Jackson." . . . with accuracy, a feat virtually unmatched: Maher and Bohls, p. 36.

88 "the key figure" in the Horns' school-record 44-game win streak.: Pennington, p. 13.

89 When the challenger meets the champion, . . . Darrell Royal and his top-ranked Longhorns.: Bill Little, "Bill Little Commentary: The Anatomy of a Challenge," *TexasSports.com*, Oct. 24, 2004, http://www.texassports.com/sports/m-footbl/spec-rel/102404aab.html.

89 The so-called experts even . . . were "at best apprehensive.": Little, "The Anatomy of a Challenge."

89 they were quietly going about the . . . stability in the time of possession.: Little, "The Anatomy of a Challenge."

89 "We're ready.": Little, "The Anatomy of a Challenge."

90 Texas fans lit up radio talk . . . "He prepared himself well this week.": Suzanne Halliburton, "Redeemed," *Austin American-Statesman*, Oct. 14, 2001.

90 "Of course this feels great," . . . both his team and to himself.: Halliburton, "Redeemed."

90 It's redemption, but at the same time, we're not going to be satisfied.: Halliburton, "Redeemed."

91   A cousin had a hot tip for his coaching kin at Texas.: Kirk Bohls, "Horns Harvest Bountiful Scorer in Freshman Schreiber," *Austin American-Statesman*, Jan. 14, 2002.

91   "at least an hour's tractor drive . . . "The gym," she said.: Bohls, "Horns Harvest Bountiful Scorer."

91   with its full complement of 119 students: Olin Buchanan, "Schreiber's Performance Leaves No Doubt," *Austin American-Statesman*, Jan. 6, 2002.

91   From the fourth grade on, . . . her family's 100 Holstein cows: Bohls, "Horns Harvest Bountiful Scorer."

91   The number of people at UT. . . . I was not used to that at all.: "Parting Thoughts with Heather Schreiber," *TexasSports.com*, http://www.texassports.com/sports/w-volley/spec-rel/120505aab.html.

92   Dillon went into the game as a . . . "I was pretty amazed,": Suzanne Halliburton, "Many Happy Returns," *Austin American-Statesman*, Oct. 29, 1990, p. D1.

92   When he was 10, he lost . . . to protect his good eye.: Halliburton, "Many Happy Returns."

92   The first play I ever played, . . . I made a pretty good impression.: Halliburton, "Many Happy Returns."

93   The problem was located deep within . . . getting to it to treat it.: Little, *Stadium Stories*, p. 117.

93   "I used to be a thug . . . I said, 'Lord, lift me up.'": Bruce Newman, "'Just Born to Be Great,'" *Sports Illustrated Presents Texas Longhorns Football* (New York City: Time Inc. Home Entertainment, 2009), p. 56.

93   "a part of me, just like the clothes . . . and I say a prayer.": Little, *Stadium Stories*, p. 117.

93   Earl, when you get in that end zone, act like you have been there before.: Little, *Stadium Stories*, p. 119.

94   but ran into trouble when it lost $200 in the 1906-07 season.: Little, *Hoop Tales*, p. 3.

94   it lacked good lighting and had no heat, but it was dry.: Little, *Hoop Tales*, p. 13.

94   the team played its games in the Scottish Rite Theatre, renting the place for $75 a night,: Little, *Hoop Tales*, p. 3.

94   an arrangement that ended after the 1912-13 season.: Little, *Hoop Tales*, p. 9.

95   During the 1943, season, Coach Dana . . . "He was such a big man on campus.": Brad Townsend, "How a 5-Foot Waterboy at Texas Became a Football Icon," *The Dallas Morning News*, July 22, 2001, http://www.dallasnews.com/sharedcontent/dws/spt/colleges/texas/stories/012208.

95   His heart is way bigger than he is.: Townsend.

96   Every time he got the call, he'd pump up and go out there." Bill Little, "Bill Little Commentary: Large Leo Leaves Too Soon," *TexasSports.com*, April 6, 2002, http://www.texassports.com/sports/m-footbl/spec-rel/050702aab.html.

96   He stood 6-foot-6 and . . . a back-up offensive lineman in 1968.: Little, "Large Leo Leaves Too Soon."

96   Sooners were moving in for . . . then on, he was a defensive tackle.: Little, "Large Leo Leaves Too Soon."

96   when he answered the call by . . . He was pretty sick.": Little, "Large Leo Leaves Too Soon."

96   Leo Brooks is trustworthy. He gives a good effort all the time.: Little, "Large Leo Leaves Too Soon."

97   When the 7-2 Horns left for . . . with "We believe" on the front.": Bill Little: "Bill Little Commentary: Visions of the Fall," *TexasSports.com*, Nov. 4, 2007, http://www.texassports.com/sports/m-footbl/spec-rel/110407aad.html.

97   "Visions of their South Division . . . heads of the faithful in Stillwater.": Little, "Visions of the Fall."

97   Faith is a strong and powerful thing.: Little, "Visions of the Fall."

98   "one of the few players in this country that can take over a match on her own.": Alan Trubow, "In Good Hands," *Austin American-Statesman*, Dec. 19, 2009.

98   One evening, she walked into her parents' . . . looked at his daughter, and smiled.: Trubow, "In Good Hands."

98   Always good to wake up to the sight of my baby girl.: Trubow, "In Good Hands."

99   Tommy Nobis was worried after a high-school . . . couldn't do passing work there, she said.: Bob St. John, "Roping Steers Won't Be Easy with Nobis Roaming the Range," *Echoes of Texas Football*, ed. Ken Samelson (Chicago: Triumph Books, 2006), p. 54.

99   "the finest two-way player I have ever seen." "Tommy Nobis," *Wikipedia, the free encyclopedia*, http://en.wikipedia.org/wiki/Tommy_Nobis, Sept. 20, 2010.

99   "My grades weren't so good.": St. John, p. 54.

99   He seriously considered going to Baylor "because its smaller classes were less intimidating.": Maher and Bohls, p. 155.

99   He told himself that if he didn't . . . I know my career is football.": St. John, p. 54.

99   He came close to flunking out . . . and I just lived with tutors,": Maher and Bohls, p. 155.

99   I was an average student. Football was my whole thing. That's my biggest regret today.: Maher and Bohls, p. 155.

100   In April 1885, Southwestern University . . . went with orange and white.: Jim Nicar, "University of Texas Traditions: Burnt Orange and White," *TexasSports.com*, http://www.texassports.com/trads/burnt-orange-white.html.

100   The bright orange faded, . . . Longhorn football players as 'yellowbellies.': Maher and Bohls, p. 70.

BIBLIOGRAPHY

Barnhouse, Wendell. "Streak Busters." *Big12Sports.com*. 22 Jan. 2011. http://www.big12sports.com/ViewArticle.

Bean, Peter. "Catching Up with Cat Osterman." *Burnt Orange Nation*. 3 Jan. 2011. http://www.burntorangenation.com/2011/1/3/1911256/catching-up-with-cat-osterman.

"Before There was a Longhorn, There were . . . Dogs, Pigs, and Billy Goats?: A Dog Named Pig." *Burnt Orange Living*. 22 March 2010. http://burntorangeliving.wordpress.com/tag/texas-baseball.

"Before There was a Longhorn, There were . . . Dogs, Pigs, and Billy Goats?: Clark's Billy Goat Hill." *Burnt Orange Living*. 22 March 2010. http://burntorangeliving.wordpress.com/tag/texas-baseball.

Bohls, Kirk. "Good Fella." *Echoes of Texas Football: The Greatest Stories Ever Told*. Ed. Ken Samelson. Chicago: Triumph Books, 2006. 68-73.

---. "His Strong Faith Carries Hall in Football, Life." *Austin American-Statesman*. 18 Oct. 2007. C01.

---. "Horns Harvest Bountiful Scorer in Freshman Schreiber." *Austin American-Statesman*. 14 Jan. 2002.

Buchanan, Olin. "Schreiber's Performance Leaves No Doubt." *Austin American-Statesman*. 6 Jan. 2002.

---. "She's Purrfect: Cat Osterman Fans 17 in Notching Seventh Career Perfect Game." *Austin American-Statesman*. 22 May 2005.

Cantu, Rick. "Game, Set, Match, Switch: UT Player Swaps Out Nets." *Austin American-Statesman*. 5 Feb. 2011. C01.

---. "Kathleen Nash Known for Toughness in UT Career That's About to End." *Austin American-Statesman*. 1 March 2011.

"College Football: Duke's Day." *Time*. 10 Jan. 1964. http://www.time.com/time/magazine/article/0,9171,875532-1,00.html.

Dahlberg, Bruce T. "Anger." *The Interpreter's Dictionary of the Bible*. Nashville: Abingdon Press, 1962. Vol. 1. 135-37.

Dienhart. Tom. "Leapin' Longhorns." *Echoes of Texas Football: The Greatest Stories Ever Told*. Ed. Ken Samelson. Chicago: Triumph Books, 2006. 40-43.

England, Natalie. "Texas Student-Athlete Spotlight: Sarah Lancaster." *Big12Sports.com*. 6 Jan. 2011. http://www.big12sports.com/View/Article.dbml?DB_OEM_ID=10410&ATCLID=205072.

Evans, Wilbur and Bill Little. *Texas Longhorn Baseball: Kings of the Diamond*. Huntsville, AL: The Strode Publishers, 1983.

Finger, Mike. "Comeback Hooked for UT in Alamo Bowl." *San Antonio Express-News*. 29 Dec. 2012. http://www.mysanantonio.com/sports/alamo_bowl/article/Comeback.

Funk, Joe, and Rob Doster, eds. *Texas Pride: Longhorn Glory Shines Through an Unforgettable Championship Season*. Chicago: Triumph Books, 2006.

Garber, Greg. "Seniors, Anger, Fuel First Perfect Season." *ESPN.com*. 28 Feb. 2009.: http://sports.espn.go.com/ncw/news/story?page=garber_perfect_texas.

Golden, Cedric. "It Was So Long -- Horns' 25-Inning Epic One for the Record Books." *Austin American-Statesman*. 1 June 2009. A01.

---. "National Champions 2005 Texas Longhorns: Horns Suffered Some Blows But Delivered Biggest Hits." *Austin American-Statesman*. 28 June 2005.

---. "Six Flags of Texas: Longhorns Finish CWS Unbeaten to Claim Another National Crown." *Austin American-Statesman*. 27 June 2005.

Halliburton, Suzanne. "Ain't That a Kick." *Austin American-Statesman*. 6 Dec. 2009. C01.

---. 'An Emphatic 43rd." *Austin American-Statesman*. 22 Nov. 2009. C01.

---. "Campbell's Memories of Irish at Fore This Week." *Austin American-Statesman*. 18 Sept. 1995. D1.

---. "Many Happy Returns: Former Safety Dillon Was Deadly When Foes Punted." *Austin American-Statesman*. 29 Oct. 1990. D1.

---. "Redeemed: Simms' Five TD Passes Bury OU Nightmare." *Austin American-Statesman*. 14 Oct. 2001.

---. "Scrawny Kid, Hefty Hopes: All-American Proves Size Isn't Everything." *Austin American-Statesman*. 11 Nov. 1991. D1.

Hawthorne, Bobby. *Longhorn Football: An Illustrated History*. Austin: University of Texas Press, 2007.

Hersch, Hank. "A Texas Waltz in Tennessee." *Sports Illustrated*. 21 Dec. 1987. http://sportsillustated.cnn.com/vault/article/magazine/MAG1066871/index.htm.

Jenkins, Dan. "A Gamble in the Closing Moments Gave Texas a Cotton Bowl Win Over Notre Dame and Another National Title." *Sports Illustrated Presents Texas Longhorns Football*. New York City: Time Inc. Home Entertainment, 2009. 33.

"Laura Wilkinson - 'Do It for Hilary.'": http://sports.jrank.org/pages/5303/Wilkinson-Laura--Do-Hilary.html.

Layden, Tim. "Underdogs to the Cornhuskers, The Longhorns, Led by Coach John Mackovic and QB James Brown, 'Shocked the World.'" *Sports Illustrated Presents Texas Longhorns Football*. New York

City: Time Inc. Home Entertainment, 2009. 39.

---. "Vince Young Will Not Let Up." *Sports Illustrated Presents Texas Longhorns Football.* New York City: Time Inc. Home Entertainment, 2009. 63-65.

LeBlanc, Pamela. "Launching a New Sport: Texas Built Rowing Program, and Its Athletes, from Scratch." *Austin American-Statesman.* 1 May 2002.

Little. Bill. "Bill Little Commentary: A Rose-Colored Miracle." *TexasSports.com.* 2 Jan. 2005. http://www.texassports.com/sports/m-footbl/spec-rel/010205aaa.html.

---. "Bill Little Commentary: A Touch of Class." *TexasSports.com.* 17 Dec. 2001. http://www.texassports.com/sports/m-footbl/spec-rel/121701aaa.html.

---. "Bill Little Commentary: Colt McCoy -- Memorial Day Rescue." *TexasFootball.com.* 8 June 2006. http://www.mackbrown-texasfootball.com/sports/m-footbl/spec-rel/060806aaa.html.

---. "Bill Little Commentary: Harrison Stafford Dies, Second Hall of Famer Passes. *TexasSports.com.* 2 Dec. 2004. http://www.texassports.com/sports/m-footbl/spec-rel/120204aaa.html.

---. "Bill Little Commentary: Honoring a Champion." *TexasSports.com.* 7 May 2002. http://www.texassports.com/sports/m-fotobl/spec-rel/050702aab.html.

---. "Bill Little Commentary: Hugh Wolfe -- The First of Many." *TexasSports.com.* 26 April 2007. http://www.texassports.com/sports/m-footbl/spec-rel/042607aab.html.

---. "Bill Little Commentary: Large Leo Leaves Too Soon." *TexasSports.com.* 6 April 2002. http://www.texassports.com/sports/m-footbl/spec-rel/050702aab.html.

---. "Bill Little Commentary: Momma's Roses." *TexasSports.com.* 3 Aug. 2009. http://www.texassports.com/sports/m-footbl/spc-rel/080309aab.html.

---. "Bill Little Commentary: The Anatomy of a Challenge." *TexasSports.com.* 24 Oct. 2004. http://www.texassports.com/sports/m-footbl/spec-rel/102404aab.html.

---. "Bill Little Commentary: The Learning Curve." *TexasSports.com.* 13 Sept. 2004. http://www.texassports.com/sports/m-footbl/spec-rel/091304aab.html.

---. "Bill Little Commentary: The Quarterback's Tale." *TexasSports.com.* 1 Nov. 2007. http://www.texassports.com/sports/m-footbl/spec-rel/110107aad.html.

---. "Bill Little Commentary: Visions of the Fall." *TexasSports.com.* 4 Nov. 2007. http://www.texassports.com/sports/m-footbl/spec-rel/110407aad.html.

---. "Bill Little Commentary: Wait Just a Second." *TexasSports.com.* 18 Dec. 2009. http://www.texassports.com/sports/m-footbl/spec-rel/121809aaa.html.

---. "Bill Little Commentary: When the Shouting Has Gone." *TexasSports.com.* 10 Oct. 2008. http://www.texassports.com/sports/m-footbl/spec-rel/101008aab.html.

---. "Bill Little Commentary: While You Were Sleeping." *TexasSports.com.* 7 Sept. 2008. http://www.texassports.com/sports/m-footbl/spec-rel/090708aah.html.

---. *Hoop Tales: Texas Longhorns Men's Basketball.* Guilford, CN: The Globe Pequot Press, 2008.

---. *Stadium Stories: Texas Longhorns.* Guilford, CN: The Globe Pequot Press, 2005.

---. *Texas Football: Yesterday & Today.* Lincolnwood, IL: West Side Publishing, 2009.

"Longhorn Hall of Honor: Laura Wilkinson." *TexasSports.com.* 17 Nov. 2009. http://www.texassports.com/genrel/111709aab.html.

MacArthur, John. *Twelve Ordinary Men.* Nashville: W Publishing Group, 2002.

Maher, John. "Handling Life's Overhead Smashes." *Austin American-Statesman.* 23 May 1993. C1.

---. "In 1918, UT's Football Foes Included War, Flu Pandemic." *Austin American-Statesman.* 3 May 2009. A01.

Maher, John and Kirk Bohls. *Long Live the Longhorns: 100 Years of Texas Football.* New York City: St. Martin's Press, 1993.

Murphy, Austin. "With a Stunning Comeback Victory, Vince Young and the Longhorns Set the Tone for a Magical Season." *Sports Illustrated Presents Texas Longhorns Football.* New York City: Time Inc. Home Entertainment, 2009. 41.

Nasits, Emily. "Earl Campbell: The College Years." *Echoes of Texas Football: The Greatest Stories Ever Told.* Ed. Ken Samelson. Chicago: Triumph Books, 2006. 60-67.

"National Championship Moments: 1995 Women's Tennis." *TexasSports.com.* http://www.texassports.com/sports-w-tennis/spec-real/120406aaa.html.

Newman, Bruce. "'Just Born to Be Great.'" *Sports Illustrated Presents Texas Longhorns Football.* New York City: Time Inc. Home Entertainment, 2009. 55-57.

Nicar, Jim. "The Origins of 'The Eyes of Texas.'" *Longhorn Band/University of Texas at Austin: History of School and Fight Songs.* http://mbe187.music.utexas.edu/Longhorn band/History/Songs.aspx.

---. "The Rose Bowl That Was (Almost) in Austin." 21 Dec. 2009. http://www.utexas.edu/know/2009/12/21/rose_bowl_almost.

---. "University of Texas Traditions: Burnt Orange and White." *TexasSports.com.* http://www.texassports.com/trads/burnt-orange-white.html.

"Parting Thoughts with Heather Schreiber." *TexasSports.com.* http://www.texassports.

com/sports/w-volley/spec-rel/120505aab.html.

Pennington, Richard. *Longhorn Hoops: The History of Texas Basketball*. Austin: University of Texas Press, 1998.

Price, Asher. "Texas Longhorns: National Champions, Party!" *Austin American-Statesman*. 16 Jan. 2006.

Putnam, Pat. "A Little Texas Ingenuity Proved to Be the Difference Against Favored Alabama in the Cotton Bowl." *Sports Illustrated Presents Texas Longhorns Football*. New York City: Time Inc. Home Entertainment, 2009. 35.

"Randy McEachern: Profile." *TexasSports.com*. http://www.texassports.com/genrel/mceachern_randy00.html.

Richardson, Steve. *Tales from the Texas Longhorns: A Collection of the Greatest Stories Ever Told*. Champaign, IL: Sports Publishing L.L.C., 2003.

"Ricky Williams: What It Means to Be a Longhorn." *TexasSports.com*. 26 June 2008. http://www.texas sports.com/sports/m-footbl/spec-rel/062608aaa.html.

Riggs, Randy. "Barnes' Hungry Horns Hold Court in All Seasons." *Austin American-Statesman*. 18 June 2000. C1.

Robbins, Kevin. "At the End of Journey Never Begun, Peace." *Austin American-Statesman*. 25 Nov. 2010. A01.

---. "Young Was the Hero, But Robison's Stop Helped Deliver Horns' 2005 Title." *Austin American-Statesman*. 31 Dec. 2009. http://www.statesman.com/sports/longhorns/young-was-the-hero-but-robisons-stop-helped-157871.html.

Roser, Mary Ann and Mark Rosner. "UT 40 -- Missouri 10: Big 12's Stormy Start." *Austin American-Statesman*. 1 Sept. 1996. A1.

Rosner, Mark. "A Study in Persistence." *Austin American-Statesman*. 12 Dec. 2007. C01.

---. "Gregory Has Been Good to Howdens." *Austin American-Statesman*. 1 Sept. 2004.

Royal, Darrell with John Wheat. *Coach Royal: Conversations with a Texas Football Legend*. Austin: University of Texas Press, 2005.

St. John, Bob. "Roping Steers Won't Be Easy with Nobis Roaming the Range." *Echoes of Texas Football: The Greatest Stories Ever Told*. Ed. Ken Samelson. Chicago: Triumph Books, 2006. 52-54.

Schoor, Gene. *100 Years of Texas Longhorn Football*. Dallas: Taylor Publishing Co., 1993.

Sharpe, Wilton. *Longhorn Madness: Great Eras in Texas Football*. Nashville. Cumberland House, 2006.

Stratton, W.K. *Backyard Brawl: Inside the Blood Feud Between Texas and Texas A&M*. New York City: Three Rivers Press, 2003.

Swanson, Mark. "Final Four Is Better Late Than Never for UT's Dickson." *Austin American-Statesman*. 16 Dec. 2010. C01.

Terrell, Roy. "Kickoff in Dixie." *Sports Illustrated*. 29 Sept. 1958. http://sportsillustrated.cnn.com/vault/article/magazine/MAG1002884/index.htm.

"Terrence Rencher: Completing a Journey.": *TexasSports.com*. 8 Dec. 2007. http://www.texassports.com/sports/m-baskbl/spec-rel/120807aaa.html.

"Tom Campbell Profile." *TexasSports.com*. http://www.texassports.com/genrel/campbell_tom00.html.

"Tommy Nobis." *Wikipedia, the free encyclopedia*. http://en.wikipedia.org/wiki/Tommy_Nobis.

"Top 100 Moments in Texas Men's Basketball History." *TexasSports.com*. http://www.texassports.com/sports/m-baskbl/spec-rel/top-100-moments.html.

Townsend, Brad. "How a 5-Foot Waterboy at Texas Became a Football Icon." *The Dallas Morning News*. 22 July 2001. http://www.dallasnews.com/sharedcontent/dws/spt/colleges/texas/stories/012208.

Trubow, Alan. "In Good Hands." *Austin Statesman-American*. 19 Dec. 2009.

Van Deusen, Amy. "Q&A with Olympic Champion Laura Wilkinson." *Women's Health*. http://www.womenshealthmag.com/fitness/laura-wilkinson-interview.

Wangrin, Mark. "Horns Pick and Bruise: Humphrey Lets Imagination Run Wild in Snagging 3 Interceptions, and Williams Just Runs Wild." *Austin American-Statesman*. 6 Sept. 1997. C1.

---. "It Pours, and Texas Reigns." *Austin American-Statesman*. 1 Sept. 1996. C1.

---. "Texas' Softball Dream Will Get Real Today." *Austin American-Statesman*. 15 Feb. 1996. D2.

LONGHORNS

INDEX
(LAST NAME, DEVOTION DAY NUMBER)